Spiritual Direction
and the Gay Person

Spiritual Direction and the Gay Person

JAMES L. EMPEREUR SJ

GEOFFREY
CHAPMAN

Geoffrey Chapman
A Cassell imprint
Wellington House, 125 Strand, London WC2R 0BB

www.cassell.co.uk

© James L. Empereur SJ 1998

First published 1998

British Library Cataloguing-in-Publication Data
A catalogue record for this book is available from the British Library.

ISBN 0–225–66831–9

Typeset by Keystroke, Jacaranda Lodge, Wolverhampton
Printed and bound in Great Britain by Biddles Ltd, Guildford and King's Lynn

Contents

To Shane Martin with gratitude and affection

Introduction

When I first mentioned to colleagues and friends that I was considering writing a book on spiritual direction with gay people, the response was universally the same, that there is a definite need for such a book at this time. Further consultation produced the same reaction. A visit to the larger bookstores will reveal a definite section devoted to gay/lesbian studies. The literature on women's issues is larger but the gay/lesbian literature is now considerable. This is especially true in regard to what we call self-help books. The shelves are filled with titles concerned with such topics as 'coming out', the experience of being in the closet, the family dynamics in the lives of gay men and lesbians, and the joy of gay sex. Most of this literature is of the affirmative kind, helping gay men and lesbians through stories, biographies and social analysis to be more self-accepting, more self-loving and more able to negotiate in a homophobic environment.

Among this varied collection the reader will find a few books of philosophical, psychological and theological depth. But they are not many. Those titles which indicate an interest in the spiritual lives of homosexuals need careful evaluation since 'spirituality' is made to refer to a vast amount of things. Finally, there is a growing repertory of gay/lesbian literature. Many of the most profound reflections on the gay/lesbian experience are found in these novels, plays, short stories and poems. This literary source seems to have real promise for the development of a gay/lesbian spirituality. The field where feminist investigation clearly is ahead of gay/lesbian studies is that of theology. There has been some quite respectable research done in homosexuality and the Bible and Western church history, but nothing which can rank with the feminist critique of Scripture and of the history of Western thought. We need more time pondering over the gay/lesbian experience in order to develop these more in-depth studies, and we need more people, especially gays and lesbians, to devote their scholarship and the fruit of their reflection on their experience to make the application to Scripture, theology and spirituality. Lesbians seem to have a slight edge over gay men here because they also participate in the larger on-going feminist world of research and reflection.

I offer this volume as one attempt to move gay/lesbian studies into the field of spirituality in a concrete way. It is not meant as an intro-ductory book on spiritual direction nor is it a self-help book for homosexuals. Its primary audience is spiritual directors and directees, especially of the Christian faith, many of whom are certainly not novices in the spiritual life. But it is not limited to these people. There is much here that any gay man or woman who is interested in the spiritual journey would find helpful. It is not only Christian directors who offer spiritual direction; many others do so under a more secular, psycho-logical guise. These directors and their directees are not simply engaging in psychological counselling because they do wish to be in contact with the transcendent aspects of human living. They may share many of the beliefs of their explicitly Christian brothers and sisters. The fact is that they may have little specific religious commitment in terms of the Christian denominations. They may belong to the unchurched. They may be committed Jews, Buddhists, Hindus, Sikhs, or members of one or other of the host of religious traditions. There are many people who seem to have few religious beliefs but are on a journey which is in fact quite spiritual. It is now a truism, but no less true, that there are many who are seeking a spiritual life outside the institutional Church. My focus on my main audience is clear: the gay/lesbian Christian spiritual directees and their directors. But all the categories referred to above could find something in this volume which would be helpful for them in their spiritual quests.

As is already obvious I am not rigidly consistent in my use of terms regarding homosexuals. I refer interchangeably to homosexuals, gay/lesbian, gay men and lesbian women, gay people, and gay men and women. These terms should be clear enough. The only possible confusion would come from my use of the word 'gays' alone. For me clearly it means both men and women. However, I also use 'gays/lesbians' where 'gays' refers only to men. This more fluid use of these terms should not be an insurmountable obstacle. Others would prefer something more clearly consistent. Some prefer never to use the word 'homosexuals', seeing it as a medical term. But that seems unrealistic in the present world. People also use the word without placing on it a medical or even moral evaluation. I do not believe that we have reached that degree of maturity where we can say that certain of these terms have reached such classic status that they are to be used to the exclusion of others. Many would not agree.

Certain other qualifications are necessary. This book does not adopt an advocacy position regarding specific civil rights of gays or the morality of homosexual activity. In fact, the only thing advocated is how to assist the gay man and lesbian woman in their spiritual pursuits. What is said about gay rights or ecclesiastical positions is put forward only as part of a project dedicated to making it possible for gays and lesbians to follow their conscience as best as they know how in their spiritual journey. If the reader detects a certain slant more to the homosexual male than the homosexual female, it is because the writer is a man. I believe what I have developed will be of great assistance to lesbians committed to the spiritual life. But I am equally sure that a woman writing such a book would give it a different flavour and emphasis. Lesbians and those who work with them will need to make such adjustments when they make use of the book.

Because this is not an advocacy book in the way a book on moral theology or politics might be and because I cast the net fairly wide as regards the audience, individuals holding certain clear positions on homosexuality may be uncomfortable with the way certain points are articulated. They might prefer something more definitive. That might be possible if this were a book written by a Roman Catholic for other Roman Catholics only. But I am interested in providing some help to those directors and directees who are not Roman Catholics but belong to some other denomination, those who participate in the life of a religious tradition other than that of Christianity, and those who lead highly spiritual lives but who do not fit into the known religious traditions.

This means that it is not possible to present one position on homosexuality for this variety of directors and directees and try to impose it upon them. This is not a book on confessional counselling. Later I make some distinctions between being a confessor and being a spiritual director. It might be possible to insist on a certain position in confession but in spiritual direction it would only alienate the directee, who might well end the relationship, and so any possibility of assisting that person spiritually would be lost. As media reports make clear, there are those who think the whole world should come around to their ethical position on homosexuality, whether this be the mainline Christian denominations, the Christian Right, or those supporting same-sex unions. I do not think that a clear consensus is taking place nor do I expect it to happen soon. In the meantime I want to provide some directions and insights for a variety of gay men and women in their struggles to find God in their lives.

When I use the phrase, homosexual (or gay/lesbian) experience, I am not presuming the presence of genital activity. It may be part of the experience, past and/or present, but the same moral evaluation should not be placed on the whole experience of being gay that one might place on genital activity specifically. The distinction between homosexual orientation and homoerotic acts is widely known. Moreover, when we speak of masculine and feminine heterosexual experience we do not necessarily imply that the person is sexually active. It is only because there is such sensitivity and conflict around the area of homosexuality today that I feel constrained to make such obvious qualifications.

I am indebted to all the gay men and women who have come to me for spiritual direction over the years. I have learned from them and they are part of this book. There are others who for some time have contributed to my deeper understanding of gay/lesbian spirituality and many of them need to remain nameless. I am particularly grateful to those who reviewed the manuscript in one or other of its several stages and have enhanced the book through their wisdom. So, a special thanks to John Baldovin SJ, Richard Hardy, Peter Gray SS, Cornelius Hubbuch CFX, Kenneth Landry, Shane Martin, Maurice Monette, Arturo Perez, Xavier John Seubert OFM and Michael Walsh. I am also grateful to Thomas McElligott for his painstaking search for many of my references.

1

The gift of gay spirituality in spiritual direction

Homosexuality in a new key

Homosexuality is one of God's most significant gifts to humanity. To be gay or lesbian is to have received a special blessing from God. All humans receive their own special graces from their creator, but God has chosen some to be gay and lesbian as a way of revealing something about God-self that heterosexuals do not.[1] On the acceptance of this premise all authentic and successful spiritual direction with gays and lesbians stands or falls. A spiritual director who cannot embrace it would be advised to limit his/her work with homosexuals. This does not mean that the director must accept everything which passes as gay/lesbian activity. It does not imply that the director cannot adhere to his/her Church's position on the morality of homoerotic activity. But it does mean that a director who wishes to devote considerable time to the direction of homosexuals ought not to see that particular orientation as something less than the heterosexual one.[2]

All aware and sensitive directors know that when someone comes to them for accompaniment in their spiritual journey, taking them into confidence about some of the most significant parts of their personal stories, they are in the presence of their God made manifest in the human form of the directee. Some directors may also sense that when that person is homosexual that God is present in a homosexual way. Such an attitude is the bottom line for authentic work with gays and lesbians. Nothing less can be expected of the director.[3]

Homosexual and holy are not incompatible terms. James Cotter has made the point that one of the greatest obstacles to affirming the holiness of the homosexual is the emphasis on the term 'unnatural' when speaking of gay and lesbian relationships. Cotter reminds us that the term is not self-evident. In fact, for directors who do considerable gay and lesbian direction there will come the time (and more than once) when, despite their own reservations about same-sex relationships, they must ask the same question as does Cotter: how are these same-sex relationships a means of grace for the persons involved and how is it that people who live in such unions move towards sainthood through the struggles which are particular to them?[4]

Each directee, whether gay or straight, is an epiphany of God in some way. Each directee is a sexual person. As such, each directee will manifest something about the creative love and life-giving power of God. Because, as far as we know, the majority of people in the world are heterosexual, the sexuality of most human beings reaches a special fulfilment, a high degree of sacramentality, in the conception and birth of another human being.[5] For most directors that means they will be dealing with heterosexuals who have the capacity and disposition to be our most frequent examples of this creative love and life-giving power of God.[6]

If that is the case, what then of gay/lesbian persons? How are they a manifestation of that love and power of God? They do it in a *special* way.[7] That is why their sexuality is a charism among their brothers and sisters. Christian gays possess a charism which is analogous to the charism of a religious vocation.[8] Members of religious orders and congregations are not the only Christians called to live lives which are chaste, poor and obedient in the gospel sense of these virtues. All Christians are. Religious are few in number and they are few because they are asked to live this life with a certain intensity and reservation in response to a call. This call which makes them different, but no better, than other Christians is named a charism. Where the gay man's charism differs from that of the charism of a male member of a religious order is that the gay's charism is a sexual charism. Just as God has given a certain gift to priests, brothers or sisters in religious life to follow the gospel with a certain public character, so God has given to gay men or lesbian women a special sexual gift which shows forth the diversity and beauty of God in our world in a public way. All creatures of God show forth God's handiwork, but the world also needs variation so that the richness of this handiwork is made unmistakably evident. God gives gays and lesbians the rather startling variation of their sexuality to help their brothers and sisters have greater insights into the reality of their God.[9]

The comparison of the charism of gays and lesbians with religious life is not a complete analogy. Religious life is a call over and above the call we receive from God in our being created a son or daughter of God. Gay sexuality is a fact of creation. The similarity of charism is based on the liminality of the experience. Religious are few in terms of the total population and are asked to live in a certain way which carries with it a certain counter-cultural quality. If religious life is indistinguishable from the rest of the Christian life, there seems to be no purpose for its existence. The major transitions through which religious life is now going in an effort to discover its place in the world today is proof of this.

Homosexuals, too, are a minority. They, too, must live counter-cultural lives. Later I shall argue that they must lead these more marginal, more liminal lives to make a contribution to humanity. Unlike religious men and women they had no choice about their call. They were not asked if they wanted to be homosexual. There are so many important things about ourselves as creatures which have been given to us: our gender, our orientation, our colour. We did not choose our parents, our nationality, our particular gifts and limitations. Charism is not primarily based on choice but upon a gift given to someone to be shared because the world needs the presence of that gift. To put it in theological language, just as for the holy and healthy religious so for the healthy and holy gay/lesbian there should be a more obvious eschatological character to their lives. That is, their call is to remind the world of something it might too easily overlook. All charisms converge in the task of raising up the God hidden in our world and our lives.

Sexuality and spirituality

It would be difficult to affirm the goodness of the homosexual orientation were sexuality and spirituality still at odds with each other. The separation of the two because of the body/soul dualism is well known and well documented in the history of the Western world.[10] James Nelson who has written widely in the area of sexuality and spirituality claims that a shift is taking place which is reintegrating the two.[11] He sees that the move to experience in theology has changed the basic question in

Christianity from: 'what do the Bible, tradition and the Church say about sexuality?' to 'what does our experience of sexuality say about our understanding of the faith?' The gay man cannot be content to wait for the tradition to tell him how to think and feel about God but rather he needs to ask himself how he is actually experiencing God and how his experience can contribute to the overall understanding of the God reality today.[12] Most importantly, he needs to *trust* his experience of God.

The deeper issue here is the inadequacy of the tradition to deal with advances in contemporary understanding of the human person since it is still too often based on philosophical essentialism. Contemporary moral theology has moved away from this kind of essentialism when it sees sin and grace as relational realities. The states of grace and sin are not some static conditions of our souls which can be measured as to their beginning and end. Vincent Genovesi says:

> At the deepest level of our existence our lives are lived either in grace, inspirited and informed to greater or lesser degrees of a love of God and neighbor, or they are lived in selfishness and sin, in which case we are basically living loveless lives.[13]

This means that when assessing our relationship with God we cannot merely be satisfied to ask simple questions such as: 'is this act wrong or right?' We must ask 'to what extent is my life a loving one? To what extent is there a failure to love in my life? . . . The truth seems to be that we choose to help or hurt, to love or be selfish, through numerous small decisions over a period of time.'[14]

What is often called the essentialistic tradition, that is, the one which asserts that there are absolute norms independent of historical circumstances, finds it difficult to have a positive perspective on the homosexual experience. In order to understand the nature of our sexuality we must read its history. To do so will reveal how human beings have been sexual through mutually empowering relationships or through controlling others by abusing the power over others. As thinkers such as Michel Foucault point out, our sexuality is socially constructed. It is not simply given in an unchanging form at the beginning of human creation. We were relational at our origins and we are relational today. Our identities were not fixed from the beginning. Carter Heyward puts it this way:

There is no such thing as a homosexual or a heterosexual if by this we mean to denote a fixed essence, an essential identity. There are rather homosexual and heterosexual people – people who *act* homosexually or heterosexually . . . We are only who we are becoming in relation to one another.[15]

As Heyward observes, an historical reading of our sexuality is a challenge to both gays and lesbians as well as to those who are opposed to them. Gays and lesbians cannot claim that because they *are* a certain way, they have certain rights to act in a certain way. Nor can those opposed to homosexuality claim that gays and lesbians are by their very nature flawed and disordered. The historical perspective helps us to see that it is what we *do* rather than what we *are* that is significant in the area of Christian living.[16]

Moreover, sexuality is increasingly seen as a necessary part of our spiritual lives and so intrinsic to our experience of God. This perspective sees companionship rather than procreation as the primary purpose of sexuality, something which, according to Nelson, Protestant thinkers had maintained three centuries ago. Once that premise is accepted, then, says Nelson,

the human hunger for physical and emotional intimacy is of enormous spiritual significance. It ought not to be denigrated as unbecoming to the spiritual life. Thus theology has been giving new attention to the insight that sexuality is crucial to God's design that creatures do not dwell in isolation and loneliness but in communion and community.[17]

That sexuality should be intrinsic to our experience of God should hardly come as a surprise to those Christians who take seriously an incarnational theology. Unfortunately, it does come as a surprise and to the consternation of many. But as Helminiak reminds us: 'Without sexual integration one cannot be a fully functioning person. Contemporary awareness also adds the corollary: only a fully functioning person can be spiritually developed.'[18] The challenge for the churches will be, given their past negativity regarding homosexuality, how they are called to respond to the fact that gays too must include their sexuality in their experiences of God. They, like any heterosexual, must find ways to have a fully sexual experience of God. Such a statement can be easily misunderstood because the word, sexual, for many implies an erotic, genital experience. What I mean by 'sexual' here is that total experience of oneself as a man or a woman, as straight or gay/lesbian. Our experience of sexuality as something diffused throughout our entire person refers to our self-images, our imaginations, our bodily feelings, our sense of how our gender affects our way of being. This more complete personal embodiment is often manifested in our experience of being at home in our bodies, being comfortable with being enfleshed, being happy with having genitals. In a heterosexual marriage this would usually imply genital expression.

A major part of the shift which is bringing sexuality and spirituality back together is taking place in the field of ethics. It is the movement away from an act-orientated morality to one which is more processive in character. Sinning in the area of sexuality is not so much about doing 'certain bad things' but rather acting in such a way as to become estranged from our sexuality, either by denigrating the body or by turning it into an object of worship.[19] We are more aware of such alienation today because we see how it manifests itself in the oppression of women and in sexual violence, not to mention the seemingly endless ways in which the advertising and entertainment world manipulate us for their own ends.[20] Although understandable from an historical perspective, it is still unfortunate that it has been the Church which has promoted this more act-orientated kind of morality where individual sexual actions are judged in isolation from the rest of the person as one would look at a small part of creation under a microscope, prescinding from the larger world.[21]

Christians themselves have contributed to the alienation that so many gays and lesbians feel. The summons for them is to move away from the disembodied notion of salvation which has afflicted Christianity for centuries, and find new ways to include their gay brothers and sisters in a more holistic approach to salvation. It is an approach which affirms the holiness of our most human, sexual selves. Nelson notes:

> Sexual sanctification means growth in bodily self-acceptance, in the capacity for sensuousness, in the capacity for play, in the diffusion of the erotic throughout the body (rather than in its genitalization) and in the embrace of the androgynous possibility.[22]

This is not an ideal newly conceived at the end of the twentieth century.

6

Fully human living, finding its perfection in God, has always been at the heart of Christianity. The discussions today in Christology make this clear. We cannot appreciate the full.humanity of Jesus and bracket his sexuality. As Joan H. Timmerman points out, we cannot equate the formula 'Jesus is like us in all things save sin' with 'he is like us in all thing except sex'.[23] We can easily and comfortably point to such events as the transfiguration as a manifestation of Jesus' divinity, but we do not very easily seek the epiphany of Jesus' humanity in 'the warm comfort of the genitals'.[24] Timmerman says:

> The incarnation, in a real sense, is not complete until the community of people discovers God disclosed in their own humanity, just so, an element of Christology is lacking until we can allow ourselves to formulate images of Jesus entering as deeply into the passion of sexuality as we have done regarding the passion of his suffering.[25]

It would be a contradiction for the churches to teach an incarnational spirituality where sexuality grounds our very capacity to love God, and then ask the homosexual to be in effect 'a-sexual'. Here the invitation to the churches is surely one of theological articulation and rearticulation, but perhaps the even greater challenge is that a significant change of thinking is taking place among their members often at variance with official teaching. At a time of such testing we need to listen to all in the churches to discern the voice of God. It is not beyond the workings of God that our gay and lesbian brothers and sisters are teaching us something about God in the flesh and how to live under the cross.

Finally, Nelson sees the coming together of spirituality and sexuality in the public recognition of sexuality both of the individual and the church community. He ascribes much of this to religious feminism as well as gay/lesbian consciousness. There is an acknowledgement in the churches that in the past Protestant worship was excessively suspicious of feelings and the body, that the body seemed to have no place in Catholic incarnational theology as it was being taught and practised, and that Christian education did not place sexuality firmly in the centre of the believer's journey of faith. It seems strange to put it this way, but it is as if the Church is finally realizing that all of its members have bodies with genitalia. And some of these members are gay.

It is no longer possible to treat sexuality as something private. The Church cannot, on the one hand, be very public about abortion, family planning, sexual abuse, teenage pregnancies and all the other eye-grabbing issues which are ever present in our newspapers and television and then deal with genital behaviour on solely individualistic terms. Sexual issues are as pervasive today as those of racism and economics. No wonder that many are questioning the body/spirit dualism which has held us captive for so long. For instance, a spirituality which dichotomizes the sacred and the profane is one which separates liturgy from justice and inculturation from both worship and social issues. Such separation does not work religiously speaking and we find that we cannot found a spirituality on such a chasm.[26] Today, there is a renewal of a more creation-centred spirituality. This is a name which covers a broad spectrum of spiritualities, whether that of Augustine or of Matthew Fox.[27] We are in the midst of this change and part of it is the re-introduction of sexuality to spirituality.[28] Not all is clear. Mistakes have been and will be made. But gays and lesbians must be part of this wedding of spirituality and sexuality. They can benefit from it by allowing themselves to find their sexuality as a way to God. They can contribute to it by bringing to the heterosexual world an experience of God that only they can have.[29] It is a perspective and experience needed for the full epiphany of God to take place in our time. God has created gays and lesbians for this purpose and entrusted them with this mission.

The significance of the gay experience for Christian spirituality today[30]

I believe that when the history of spirituality in the twenty-first century is written it will show the many ways in which the gay experience will have enriched both theology and spirituality. I will focus on only one such contribution, one which I think central to the future of spirituality, namely, the overcoming of a dualistic understanding and experience of the human person, of society, and of our relationship with God. It would not be facetious to say that we could write the history of Christian spirituality by examining the presence of dualisms in the Christian community. There has been and continues to be an injustice present when these particular dualisms rule our lives.

Theoretically, we are all capable of achieving the union of flesh and spirit, of advancing the working together of society and the Church, and of integrating our sexuality and our deepest experiences of prayer. But these convergences are not so easily obtained. Society, as well as the

Church, struggles with them with a varying degree of success. The division of the person into body (i.e. material) and soul (i.e. spiritual) is still alive in Christian thinking, as the experience of funerals makes clear. That is, so many people still identify the remains in the casket with the body as if the soul was some *thing* existing on its own. A more biblical, more holistic approach would understand the words, 'body' and 'soul', to refer to the whole person under the different dimensions of a way of being in the world (body) and in terms of the life-giving qualities of the person (soul). A fragmenting dualism is especially obvious in the area of sexuality. That we find it unimaginable that sexual intercourse can be a form of prayer comes home to me each time during a marriage preparation session when I ask the couple if sexual union will be part of their prayer. Some few indicate that it will; others seem puzzled by the question; some react with fear and even a kind of horror. Despite all the efforts made by spiritual writers and practitioners as well as feminists to overcome this dualistic approach we still lack the kind of integration of matter and spirit required if spirituality and sexuality are to become partners in our movement toward God.

We need to look for new paradigms and more examples of such integration. As various liberation movements have made plain, we usually find the clearest examples among those we call marginal or liminal, i.e. those people who are at the margins of society, whose lives are at the edges of the dominant culture, those whose identities are rendered ambiguous by the major institutions of the world, including the Church. As I wrote in another place:

> We find it (the overcoming of dualisms) among the poor who are unable to move, pressed down by the power of their civil and ecclesiastical superiors. They are least likely to make a dualistic chasm between their body selves and their spiritual lives. For the *whole person* is oppressed, the *whole person* is poor, the *whole person* is shoved to the margins.[31]

As I will note later, it is not only the economically poor who are in such a liminal state but also those who are minorities in some sense. Those who lives are characterized by a strong attraction to the members of the same sex belong to these liminal groups also. Many gays and lesbians are poor in relation to their sexuality. Often because they cannot have their identity and feelings validated, they resort to a kind of dualism by denying their sexual energies. They hide these feelings deep within themselves. Gay and lesbian Christians often do this because of the stance of the churches toward them. This is a form of injustice which still exists. But it is precisely here where gay spirituality can make its contribution to the spiritual tradition. I mean that it is by addressing this injustice that gays and lesbians can minister to the rest of us through their liminal status. I wrote previously:

> Today, the first step in the area of justice and gay and lesbian people is the justice they owe themselves in self-affirmation and in taking on responsibility for the choice they have made regarding a given relationship. But it is not enough to know that one is poor; one must be open with others to the truth lest such poverty becomes dehumanizing.[32]

The ministry of spiritually committed gays and lesbians is primarily a ministry of vulnerability in the pursuit of a more just Church and society and a more justice-orientated spirituality. They are already in a vulnerable position in society and Church. It is not something they must seek. They are already the object of ridicule and discrimination. Yet this vulnerability need not render them weak and dysfunctional, because in this vulnerability lies their power. Gay spirituality offers to the Christian and other spiritual traditions a particular perspective on the justice intended by God. It is not a justice achieved only through angry protests against institutions nor in rejecting a homophobic church. Real justice comes 'when one puts one's energies in living compassionate, truthful, and joyous lives'.[33] This does not mean that there is no place for prophetic voices to speak out against injustices in various ways, including demonstrations. But prophecy without love and compassion is empty.

Gays and lesbians can offer to the Church a spirituality of justice with priorities which may differ from other justice-seeking groups. Homosexuals who are sensitive to issues of social injustice would agree with other justice-minded people that there is no peace without justice and that there must be justice before peace, but they would add that there must be love before justice. This is a justice which flows from compassion rather than one based on rights or moral imperatives. It is a holistic experience of justice where the usual dualism has been tempered. It is unfortunate that today the clearest example of this wholesome compassion is found in the way the gay man, for instance, deals with those living with AIDS. The fact is that the need for another paradigm of human integration is found in the witness of liminal gay men and women of compassion as they love and care for their friends who may be enduring heart-breaking pain and facing the possible end of their lives.

It is true that the justice flowing from compassionate concern for our brothers and sisters is a call to all human beings, not just to gays and lesbians. There is a great deal that unites both feminist and the gay/lesbian movements in the urge to reconstruct society and Church along more justice-orientated lines. But there is something distinctive to homosexuals that makes such compassionate loving a most fitting paradigm of the human integration which promotes justice. It is a model of human integration that fleshes out the larger picture of spiritual *sexual* growth. Like heterosexuals, gay men and women must first love themselves before they can engage in the ministry of compassionate love for others in an authentic spiritual sense. But also for gays to love themselves they must overcome certain obstacles which do not present themselves to the straight man or the straight woman. Despite what society, Church and family may tell them, they are loveable and can love themselves just as profoundly as any straight person. And they must love themselves precisely as gay because that is how God loves them and wants them to be. Straight men can be, and frequently are, threatened by much of the feminist agenda such as its anti-patriarchal programmes, its stress on equality, and its demand for a recognition of the particular way women think and interact.[34] Feminism also threatens many men in regard to their sexuality. Yet nothing calls into question a male's self-identity as much as the fact of men loving other men and expressing that love sexually. It is perceived as an attack on the last defence of masculinity which is based on a differentiation from the feminine. In its worst form this defensiveness has degenerated into 'gay bashing'. That is why the witness of the gay man is so evocative at this time. Amy E. Dean in one of her meditations for lesbians and gay men says:

> Many heterosexuals will contend that attraction to members of the opposite sex is normal and that its primary purpose – propagation – is part of the natural order of things. The fact that other people may be attracted to members of the same sex creates an incredible dilemma for them; they don't understand how something that's so natural and normal for them isn't what everyone else wants, too.[35]

Because the gay man can be so threatening to straight men, often because he is perceived as parading publicly those aspects of sexuality that straights have suppressed in their lives, the healthy gay man can witness to human integration in significant ways. Presupposing that he can love himself and claim his goodness as given by God, he can manifest a love of self where the male is not dominating a female, where the focus is not on genitality[36] and reproduction, where the importance of diffused touch throughout the body is affirmed.[37] It is not that heterosexuals cannot also witness to this kind of integration. But they must first deal with the issues of sexism, patriarchy, and the oppression of women. For this reason it may be that gay men can more directly manifest the connection between loving others and justice-making at this time.[38] This would mean that often gay men may be better witnesses to the power of the erotic in moving us to human liberation than where eroticism is allowed full play. This statement is possible if we understand, that like sexuality itself, eroticism cannot be confined to genital activity. As Audre Lorde puts it: 'We tend to think of the erotic as an easy, tantalizing sexual arousal. I speak of the erotic as the deepest life force, a force which moves us toward living in a fundamental way.'[39]

Gay men can manifest the fundamental affinity between the erotic (in Lorde's sense) and justice because in them the erotic can find a spiritual home in their relationships. Here, those involved experience themselves as equally valuable, as sources of love, and as genuine friends. Gay men can help us to understand how the erotic has healing qualities, shapes our relationships and provides the energy for us to move in a more committed way to maintain our freeing, intimate relationships. Lorde speaks directly to this connection of justice and the erotic.

When we begin to live from within outward, in touch with the power of the erotic within ourselves, and allowing that power to inform and illuminate our actions upon the world around us, then we begin to be responsible to ourselves in the deepest sense. For we begin to recognize our deepest feelings, we begin to give up, of necessity, being satisfied with suffering and self-negation, and with the numbness which so often seems like the only alternative in our society. Our acts against oppression become integral with self, motivated and empowered from within.[40]

Gay men and lesbian women can minister to heterosexual relationships today by pointing to the qualities that must be found in married life if sexual pleasure is to be experienced as a form of spiritual bonding and of liberating communication. Today, as men and women struggle to change intimate relationships from domination to partnership, they can rediscover the emancipating connection between sex and spirituality. Gay men and women can be models of how eroticism can and must influence all of our interactions with the world and with God. Marvin M. Ellison observes:

> I am convinced that a spirituality *without* erotic passion becomes lifeless and cold. God becomes an abstraction, an idea rather than a living presence in our lives. I am searching for a Christian spirituality that acknowledges that the human calling is to make passionate love in this world, in our beds and in our institutions. To love well means to share the gift of life with zeal and great generosity and to seek right relations with all others, relations of genuine equality and mutuality, of shared power and respect.[41]

By directing their erotic energies to the area of social justice not only can the gay and lesbians experience their sexuality as a sacrament of God's love for humankind[42] but it becomes their way of discerning where justice is lacking and how they might bring about that justice realistically. 'In fact, the very power of even our most intimate and orgasmic moments simultaneously frees us from ourselves, gives us back renewed to ourselves, and spills over as that energy by which we join in the liberation of all the earth.'[43]

Homosexuals today take their place along with the other marginal groups in bringing about the good news of salvation. Latin American liberationists have placed family relationships over wealth, political power and paternalism. Feminism has brought to light how sexism has adulterated the very word of God. The new churches of the Pacific challenge the Western churches' God who is presented in colonial feeling and form. There is something prophetic in these movements. The gay/lesbians participate in this same prophetic vocation. How is that so in fact?

> What the gay and lesbian saints of our time witness to the church is the fact that holiness is a passionate business, that full sexual living

brings out the uniqueness of being an embodied person, that incarnation demands mutuality and equality also among people of the same sex, that friendship is more significant than competitive relationships, that holiness is the same as enjoying life and loving in a non-possessive way by not limiting sexuality to a few occasions but by spreading it into an ongoing experience of pleasurable love.[44]

Gay spirituality may be no more incarnational than any other Christian spirituality but that does not take away from the fact that it has a special role to perform in the Christian tradition and in living out the Christian life. Gay men and women must become missionaries to a homophobic world. Gay men in particular can show straight men (and also women to the extent applicable) that they need not divide themselves off from their feelings and live disincarnate lives, that they need not prove their worth through their accomplishments, that fear of sexuality and pleasure need not turn into anger and violence, and that they can let go of control of their lives and not feel compelled to have children in order to assure themselves of a future. Gay spirituality is an inculturated Christian spirituality because it allows the gospel to grow out of the homosexual followers of Christ.[45]

Spiritual direction as I see it[46]

Before moving into the rest of this book on spiritual direction, it is only proper that the reader have a sense on how I understand spiritual direction. Over the past decades the literature in this area has grown considerably. I would be in general agreement with most of the main points of many of the definitions of direction which are now given.[47] In addition, this is my working definition of Christian spiritual direction: *the process in which a Christian accompanies others for an extended period of time for the purpose of clarifying the psychological and religious issues in the directees so that they may move toward deeper union with God and contribute to ministry within the Christian community.*

This definition implies that the method of the director is to follow the directees but not to be led by them. According to this definition the director does not intrude in the life of the directee by issuing instructions on how to live their lives or imposing on them methods of prayer or prescribed scriptural or other religious texts. It would be destructive of the spiritual direction relationship if the director tried to impose certain religious or moral norms on the directee. Spiritual direction is not the same as the sacrament of reconciliation where we confess our sins to a priest. The spiritual director in no way represents the Church as does the priest. Advice and direction may be appropriate in the confessional or they may not be. Whereas in the sacrament we have two people who belong to the same Christian community following the same norms of the good Christian life put forth by that community, in spiritual direction the director and directee may belong to the same Christian church or they may not. A realistic example will show the difference between the ministry of the confessor and that of the director. A Roman Catholic gay man confessing to a Roman Catholic priest may be in doubt or in error about the teaching of the Roman Catholic Church regarding the morality of homoerotic acts or he may be acting contrary to that teaching. The Catholic Church sees it to be the duty of the priest to enlighten the penitent in this matter to remove any lack of knowledge or mis-understanding of what the Church considers to be sinful behaviour. The situation of spiritual direction with such a gay man is quite different. It may be relevant to inform a gay directee of the teachings of his Church regarding homosexuality, but not necessarily. The director's concern is to assist him in the areas of his life where he is seeking help in his spiritual path. It is not appropriate to pass judgement on the directee's sexual activity. It is fitting to help him clarify the meaning of these activities in his life and where they do or do not fit in the particular path he has chosen to move toward God. Directors who believe that they have a right to insist that gay directees act according to their (the directors') moral norms should not engage in spiritual direction with homosexuals. Such an attitude is considered unacceptable by most spiritual directors and those who think that way would best take up a different ministry. It has been my experience that in the majority of cases of gays and lesbians the matter of genital activity does not enter into the spiritual direction process. Or, at least, it is not a central issue. They are interested in pur-suing their relationship with God in some depth. Some are committed to the celibate way of life. Others have resolved for themselves how they are going to express themselves in situations of intimacy. Sometimes, I am left unaware of that part of their lives.

However, the director does not remain non-directive, simply listening and 'letting the Holy Spirit do the directing'. I find that both the invasive and so-called non-directive approaches are cover-ups for incompetence or the director's desire to avoid dealing with painful human issues that they often characterize as not appropriate for spiritual direction.[48]

Rather the director in the approach that I espouse is very much involved, asking clarifying questions, doing follow-up from previous sessions, making concrete suggestions along the way and before all else, listening actively.[49] This approach is therapeutic because we are dealing with the human person and spiritual growth cannot be so easily separated from psychological growth. And even at the higher levels of development there is still need for healing. It is Christian because the faith commitment is the presupposed environment and the ultimate purpose is that this redounds to the benefit of the Christian community.[50]

Some will still find this insufficiently Christian or spiritual. Usually they mean that spiritual direction should deal more with specifically spiritual issues and not so much with psychological and therapeutic ones. They think that the latter are more appropriate for pastoral counselling.[51] This usually implies that a great deal of religious rather than therapeutic language will be used in spiritual direction. I do not agree with this approach. First, I do not find it that easy to compartmentalize humanity into two realms: the spiritual and the psychological. Second, as I have already noted, these directors have a tendency to ask directees such questions as: 'Have you asked God about this?' or 'What does Jesus say about this?' Directees who have had this experience have come to me confused. And rightly so, because God expects us to use ordinary human means to discover what it is God wants and not to expect some kind of personal revelation. These means are psychological and therapeutic. Sometimes we hear directees say about their unresolved issues that they are simply living one day at a time commending themselves to the graciousness of God. This can easily be a form of avoidance. The intuition of incarnational spirituality is that we work at resolving our own issues and not pass what is our responsibility on to God. To put ourselves in a holding pattern until God gives us further instructions seems to be a form of presumption.

Often in the actual experience there is little distinction between psychological counselling and spiritual direction. Therapy too is an educative process where one can enhance one's spiritual life. It is not only intended for crisis resolution. Sometimes the differences between the two can only be found in whether one lies on a couch and the amount of the fee. One real difference is that spiritual direction must be concerned with the public arena, in particular the Christian community.

Spiritual direction cannot be simply working on our own issues. It must move us into the larger areas of church life such as matters of social justice. It must make us more aware of concerns larger than having been abused or rejected, not being able to pray, and the fear that God has abandoned us. Therapy can also move us into the public arena but it need not.

Spiritual direction is one way the Christian is assisted to make the passageway of the paschal mystery. But this passageway is a public process. We are called out of our being caught up in ourselves narcissistically. We are called out by love, love of others. The paschal mystery is not only about our own dying and rising with Christ but also the liberation of other people. Transformation in Christ is not simply a personal matter. It refers to such things as the destruction of the ecological system, the maiming of the world around us. The interior life cannot remain interior only. And so spiritual direction for gays and lesbians cannot be content only to assist them in their personal journeys to God. It must also contribute to the public acceptance of their giftedness in society, the Church, and the family. In the final chapter of the book I deal explicitly with this more public passage.

Notes

1   I believe this to be true whatever may be the origins of homosexuality, whether nurture or nature, whether in our genes or not. I reject the position which claims that we opt for being homosexual as if we choose it like we choose where we are going for our vacation. In his introduction to a series of meditations for gays and lesbians as well as for those who love them and minister to them, John Edward Lazar says:

> Being gay or lesbian is part of God's plan and a unique gift to humanity. Rather than viewing it as something to be changed or hated, properly understood within the confines of the spiritual, this orientation should be welcomed, grasped, and nurtured with the full understanding, emotional and intellectual, that it is good and does participate in the Divine Plan of creation. *Outpouring of the Spirit* (New York: Carlton Press, 1995), p. 5.

Further discussion on this matter is found in Dean Hamer and Peter Copeland, *The Science of Desire: The Search for the Gay Gene and Biology of Behaviour* (New York: Simon and Schuster, 1994). The authors deal with the implications of how we view gay and lesbian persons.

For an article which is representative of the popular expression of the unchangeability of the homosexual orientation (being gay is like being left-handed) see Letha Dawson Scanzoni, 'Can homosexuals change?', *The Other Side: Christians and Homosexuality: Dancing Toward the Light*, special issue (Philadelphia, Pa. 19144: 300 W. Apsley St, 1994).

For a brief, objective and scholarly survey of the question of the causes of homosexuality by an English author see David Leal, 'Questions about causes', in *Debating Homosexuality* (Cambridge: Grove Books, 1996), pp. 8ff.

Recently, the Roman Catholic bishops of the United States issued a pastoral letter entitled, *Always Our Children: A Pastoral Message to Parents of Homosexual Children and Suggestions for Pastoral Ministers* (in *Origins*, **27** (17) (1997)). While reaffirming the Church's position on homoerotic activity, the letter speaks of gays and lesbians in the language of giftedness. Gay and lesbian children are to be seen as part of God's design. The letter is generally viewed as an advance in that it accepts gays and lesbians in the Church and is a help in overcoming discrimination against them. For more detailed comment, see *National Catholic Reporter*, 10 October 1997, p. 9. The same newspaper carried several articles dealing with the parents of homosexuals as well as the larger pastoral issue involved in its issue of 19 September 1997.

2   For a discussion of some of the religious and moral issues which arise when counselling homosexuals and the kind of neutrality possible for the counsellor, see Chapter 7 of James Nelson, *Between Two Gardens: Reflections on Sexuality and Religious Experience* (New York: The Pilgrim Press, 1983).

3   Those directors who work with gays who have no discernible belief in God would want to consult Daniel A. Helminiak, 'Non-religious lesbians and gays facing AIDS: a fully psychological approach to spirituality', *Pastoral Psychology*, **43** (5) (1995), pp. 301–18. He develops what he calls a non-theistic spirituality. He concludes his article with these words:

> When spirituality is understood as a core human reality, every aspect of life can be credited as spiritual. Every open, honest, and loving person can be seen as on a spiritual quest. The gay experience itself, lived honestly and lovingly, in flamboyant life or in horrid death, can be acclaimed as profoundly rich, sacred, holy – spiritual. (p. 317)

4   See James Cotter, 'Homosexual and holy', *The Way*, **28** (July 1988), pp. 231–43. He gives examples of how in the past some activities were thought to be unnatural but no longer are so considered. Most of us could gives examples of how some people have considered certain actions unnatural only to have that opinion challenged and changed.

5   This does not need to imply the older idea that the primary purpose of marriage is procreation. Theologians now see that as too exclusive of other purposes as well as too biologically determinative.

6   The physical ability to have sexual intercourse and cause the conception of a child, which most gay men have, is not sufficient to be a human symbol of God's love and power. Purely physical generation does not have that kind of symbolic meaning. Something more must be going on between the man and woman than mere physical exchange. That there are gay and lesbian committed couples who adopt children and give them the love and care equal to (or even surpassing) the love and care of heterosexual parents is a fact. It is also a fact that this is the experience of a very small group of people relative to the population of the world. As far as I can

determine, the ordinary symbol of God's creative power in terms of human generation remains heterosexual marriage, understanding marriage in its full sacramental sense. That is how I would see the marriage of my own father and mother.

7   For some examples see Mark Thompson (ed.), *Gay Soul: Finding the Heart of the Gay Spirit and Nature* (San Francisco: Harper, 1994).

8   The notion of being gay as a religious vocation has been more extensively developed by Ronald E. Long in his article, 'The sacrality of male beauty and homosex: a neglected factor in the understanding of contemporary gay reality', Gary David Comstock and Susan E. Henking (eds), *Que(e)rying Religion: A Critical Anthology* (New York: Continuum, 1997), pp. 266–81. He says that being gay is 'a way of life, a way of living out and actualizing one's humanness' and 'No understanding of gay life that is blind to its religious dimension, its implicit spirituality, will be adequate' (p. 276). We should read Long with caution. He takes an advocacy position especially regarding the importance of male beauty and genital sex. He seems to be a reductionist at times. Daniel A. Helminiak addresses the topic of the vocation of gay Christians in his 'The Trinitarian vocation of the gay community', Adrian Thatcher and Elizabeth Stuart (eds), *Christian Perspectives on Sexuality and Gender* (Grand Rapids, MI: Eerdmans, 1996), pp. 318–27.

9   See page 48 of an article by a gay seminarian, 'Claiming our identity', *CMI Journal: Quiet Pools and New Strength*, **16** (Winter 1993), pp. 44–8. There is a sense in which gay and lesbian religious are gifted with the charism both of sexual difference as well as living the Christian life with a certain 'light grasp on life'.

10 The reader might consult several of the articles in Thatcher and Stuart, *Christian Perspectives*, referred to above. It would be worth the effort to spend the time becoming familiar with John Boswell's *Christianity, Social Tolerance and Homosexuality* (Chicago: University of Chicago Press, 1980). Robert McAfee Brown has a chapter on sexuality and spirituality in his *Spirituality and Liberation: Overcoming the Great Fallacy* (Philadelphia: Westminister Press, 1988).

11 James Nelson 'Reuniting sexuality and spirituality', Thatcher and Stuart, *Christian Perspectives*, pp. 213–19. What I say in this section is indebted to this article. Other books by Nelson include: *Embodiment: An Approach to Sexuality and Christian Theology* (Minneapolis: Augsburg Publishing House, 1978); *Between Two Gardens: Reflections on Sexuality and Religious Experience* (New York: The Pilgrim Press, 1983); *The Intimate Connection: Male Sexuality, Masculine Spirituality* (Philadelphia: The Westminster Press, 1988); *Body Theology* (Louisville: Westminster/John Knox Press, 1992); Nelson and Sandra P. Longfellow (eds), *Sexuality and The Sacred: Sources for Theological Reflection* (Louisville: Westminister/John Knox Press, 1994).

12 This movement to experience is motivating theologians to begin the articulation of gay and lesbian theologies. This theology is in its very initial stages but it has begun. See, for instance, Gary David Comstock, *Gay Theology Without Apology* (Cleveland: The Pilgrim Press, 1993); Virginia Ramey Mollenkott, *Sensuous Spirituality: Out from Fundamentalism* (New York: Crossroad, 1993); Mary E. Hunt, *Fierce Tenderness: A Feminist Theology of Friendship* (New York: Crossroad, 1991).

13 Vincent Genovesi, *In Pursuit of Love: Catholic Morality and Human Sexuality* (Collegeville: The Liturgical Press, 1996), p. 96.

14   *Ibid.*, p. 97. Norman Pittenger has applied this more process-orientated approach specifically to homosexuality in his book, *Time for Consent: A Christian's Approach to Homosexuality* (London: SCM Press, 1976). He concludes his chapter, 'What is man?' with these words: 'To be on the way to love, in the sense in which I have sought to describe it, constitutes (I believe) man's distinctive quality. And to be on the way to such love is to begin to *live*, in the most profound sense of that verb. Robert Southwell, the recusant poet, has a lovely sentence saying exactly this: "Not where I breathe, but where I love, I live"' (p. 33).

15   Carter Heyward, 'Notes on historical grounding: beyond sexual essentialism', Nelson and Longfellow (eds), *Sexuality and the Sacred*, pp. 9–18 (p. 11). See Michael L. Stemmeler, 'Empowerment: the construction of gay religious identities', Bjorn Krondorfer (ed.), *Male Identities in a Post Christian Culture* (New York: New York University Press, 1996), pp. 94–107.

16   Carter Heyward, *Ibid.*

17   Nelson, 'Reuniting sexuality and spirituality', p. 215.

18   Daniel Helminiak, 'Self-esteem, sexual self-acceptance, and spirituality', *Journal of Sex Education and Therapy*, **15**, (3) (1989), pp. 200–10.

19   Both director and directee could profitably review the discussions taking place in the field of ethics today by consulting such a book as Genovesi, *In Pursuit of Love*.

20   In *Defying the Darkness: Gay Theology in the Shadows* (Cleveland: The Pilgrim Press, 1997) J. Michael Clark develops a gay ethics which is in conversation with feminism.

21   William C. Spohn in an address to the Catholic Theological Society of America (6 June1997) extends this more processive approach to ethics to the reception of the Eucharist. He says the AIDS crisis caused some church communities to exclude many gay people and drug users from the Eucharist.

> [E]fforts to police the boundaries of the Eucharistic participation is the effort to determine who deserves to be at the table. If the Body of Christ is commemorated and shared at the Lord's Supper, then only those who qualify morally and ideologically are worthy to receive it. I want to argue that this effort is theologically and ethically wrongheaded. Instead of checking credentials at the altar rail, we should be reflecting on the meaning of the Eucharistic celebration itself . . . We run into trouble by taking literally what we should be taking metaphorically. (page 2 of unpublished manuscript.)

22   Nelson, 'Reuniting sexuality and spirituality', p. 216.

23   Joan H. Timmerman, 'The sexuality of Jesus and the human vocation', Nelson and Longfellow (eds), *Sexuality and the Sacred*, pp. 91–104 (p. 93).

24   *Ibid.*, p. 94. Timmerman refers to the much-discussed work of Leo Steinberg, the art historian. Steinberg has given convincing evidence that the Renaissance artists were theologizing about Jesus' humanity in their paintings and sculptures when they showed Jesus' genitals and himself or his mother pointing to them. Steinberg's argument has been reinforced by later ages' attempts to cover up the sexuality of Jesus because of their own lack of comfort in this area.

25   *Ibid.*, p. 92.

26   The issue of the relationship of the sacred to the secular has been a constant theme

in modern theology. For a brief review of the issues see Michael H. Crosby OFM CAP, 'The relationship of sacred and secular', Judith A. Dwyer and Elizabeth L. Montgomery (eds), *The New Dictionary of Catholic Social Thought* (Collegeville: The Liturgical Press, 1994), pp. 857–60.

27   See 'Creation', Michael Downey, *The New Dictionary of Catholic Spirituality* (Collegeville: The Liturgical Press, 1993), pp. 238–42, Matthew Fox, *Original Blessing* (Santa Fe: Bear, 1983) and *The Coming of the Cosmic Christ* (San Francisco: Harper and Row, 1988). For a more extensive understanding of spirituality which is based on creation see Albert J. LaChance and John E. Carroll (eds), *Embracing the Earth: Catholic Approaches to Ecology* (Maryknoll: Orbis Press, 1994).

28   As should be obvious by now I recommend Nelson's article, 'Reuniting sexuality and spirituality' to all spiritual directors and directees.

29   Articulating and developing this notion is the task of gay theology.

30   What is said in this section will be expanded upon in the remaining chapters.

31   In my article, 'A lesbian and gay spirituality: the life and liturgy of DIGNITY', *Dignity USA Journal*, **24** (1) (Winter 1992), pp. 19–25.

32   *Ibid.*, p. 21.

33   *Ibid.*

34   See for instance, Mary Belenky, Blythe Clinchy, Nancy Goldberger and Jill Tarule, *Women's Ways of Knowing: The Development of Self, Voice, and Mind* (New York: Basic Books, 1986).

35   Entry for 19 February, Amy E. Dean, *Proud to Be* (New York: Bantam Books, 1994).

36   In *The Intimate Connection* James Nelson, in his discussion of homophobia, states that he, like most heterosexual men, is concerned about potency, always being ready for sex, and fears impotence. Straight men see gays as more sexual, more potent. And while they regard gays as 'less than men', they also see them as more male because homosexuality has become a symbol of sexual energy, of potency and so, more male than they. In our patriarchal structure the male is normative, but the gay man threatens this because 'he embodies the symbol of woman'. Since many, especially straight men, presume that in gay-male sex one of the men is the receiver and so the 'woman', gay men are seen as men who are willing to submit to womanization and so a threat to patriarchal man. Also, since straight men know that gay men can make them into sexual objects, this reminds straight men that they often treat women as sexual objects. Finally, we all seek affection and validation from our equals. Gay men receive that from other men. In our society where the relationship between men is based on competition, this is difficult for men to do. Straight men, therefore, place the burden of receiving this affirmation and support on women, whom often they do not regard as equals. All these are the reasons Nelson gives for the homophobia of straight men toward gay men. All these cause anger in the straight man. Straights are projecting on to gays their own uncomfortableness and ambiguity about their own sexuality, that is, their own sexual dualism where the world is rigidly divided between heterosexuals and homosexuals. The unhappy result, as Nelson notes, is that there is more gay-bashing than in the case of lesbians and 'male homophobia about males particularly undercuts the rich possibilities of men's friendship with other men'. See pp. 61 and 62.

See also Guy Kettlehack, 'Why we scare straight men', *Dancing Around the Volcano: Freeing Our Erotic Lives: Decoding the Enigma of Gay Men and Sex* (New York: Crown Publishers, Inc., 1996), pp. 66ff. See Stephen B. Boyd, 'Reconciliation with gay men', *The Men We Long to Be* (Cleveland: The Pilgrim Press, 1997), pp. 198–201. Boyd places overcoming the hostility of straight men toward gay men in the larger context of men loving each other as brothers.

37   Obviously, so much of what the gay man witnesses to is also done by the lesbian woman. I believe it would be better to have a woman elaborate on the ministry of lesbians in the field of spirituality.

38   I hope it is clear to the reader that in speaking about the ministry of gay men I am referring to those gays who are intentionally developing a spiritual life, who regard spiritual direction as an important element in such development, and whose lives are characterized by increasing personal and social integration. A 'ministry' of gay men who are *not* on a spiritual path is beyond the scope of this book.

39   Quoted by Amy E. Dean, *Proud to Be*, entry for 11 June.

40   'Uses of the erotic: the erotic as power', *Sister Outsider: Essays and Speeches by Audre Lorde* (Freedom, CA: Crossing Press, 1984), p. 58.

41   Marvin M. Elison, 'Sexuality and spirituality: an intimate – and intimidating – connection', Thatcher and Stuart (eds), *Christian Perspectives*, pp. 220–7 (p. 222).

42   For a discussion of how, from a sacramental point of view, creating new metaphors to understand homosexuality will help gays and lesbians experience themselves positively within the Christian tradition, see Xavier John Seubert OFM, 'The sacramentality of metaphors: reflections on homosexuality', *Cross Currents* (Spring 1991), pp. 52ff.

43   J. Michael Clark, 'Men's studies, feminist theology, gay male sexuality', Nelson and Longfellow (eds), *Sexuality and the Sacred*, pp. 216–28. This article deals in some depth with the relationship between sexuality and justice. I hope it is clear to the reader that the experience of the erotic for many gay men and women does not include genital expression because of a variety of commitments, a significant one being their participation in the life of a church which does not permit such expression.

44   Empereur, 'A lesbian and gay spirituality', p. 22.

45   In Chapter 7 of *Between Two Gardens*, Nelson addresses the need of the presence of gays and lesbians in the Church as a way of overcoming the homophobia which is present in the community of believers. He says: 'Gay men and lesbians need to know how much everyone in society will benefit from the gains in their own struggle for liberation. While it is grossly unfair to place the burden of liberating the oppressors upon the oppressed, it may be that the latter can find augmented self-assurance in knowing how deeply they are needed by the former' (p. 127).

46   The following section is taken from my book entitled *The Enneagram and Spiritual Direction: Nine Paths to Spiritual Guidance* (New York: Continuum, 1997), pp. 42ff. There are some emendations to this text and several footnotes have been added. This is done with permission from Continuum.

47   For instance, I can easily adopt as my own this definition given by Elizabeth Liebert SNJM, in her book, *Changing Life Patterns: Adult Development in Spiritual Direction* (New York: Paulist Press, 1992): 'Christian spiritual direction, then, is an

interpersonal helping relationship, rooted in the church's ministry of pastoral care. In this relationship, one Christian assists another to discover and live out in the context of the Christian community his or her deepest values and life goals in response to God's initiative and biblical mandate' (p. 8). A sampling of the various books on spiritual direction now available would include: Joseph Allen, *Inner Way: Toward A Rebirth of Eastern Christian Spiritual Direction* (Grand Rapids: Eerdmans, 1994); William A. Barry SJ, *Allowing the Creator to Deal with the Creature* (New York: Paulist Press, 1994); Tad Dunne, *Spiritual Mentoring* (HarperSanFrancisco, 1991); Tilden Edwards, *Spiritual Friend: Reclaiming the Gift of Spiritual Direction* (New York: Paulist Press, 1980); Kathleen Fischer, *Women at the Well: Feminist Perspectives on Spiritual Direction* (New York: Paulist Press, 1988); Alan Jones, *Exploring Spiritual Direction* (HarperSanFrancisco, 1982); Kenneth Leech, *Soul Friend: The Practice of Christian Spirituality* (San Francisco: Harper and Row, 1977); Francis Kelly Nemeck OMI and Marie Theresa Coombs, Hermit, *The Way of Spiritual Direction* (Wilmington: Michael Glazier, 1985).

48   For the less experienced director it would be helpful to consult a book like A. Elfin Moses and Robert O. Hawkins, Jr., *Counseling Lesbian Women and Gay Men* (Columbus: Merrill Publishing Co., 1982). In particular I suggest Chapter 8 on lesbian and gay male sexual activity to get a realistic understanding of homosexual activity free of assumptions. Also, Chapter 12 on confidentiality is worthwhile. For something on characteristics of a good director I suggest Chapter 2 of Carl R. Rogers, *Freedom to Learn* (Columbus: Charles E. Merrill Publishing Co., 1962), 'Being in relationship'. Another book to consult is Howard Stone, *Theological Context for Pastoral Caregiving: Word in Deed* (New York: Haworth Pastoral Press, 1966).

49   See Charles Hefling (ed.), *Our Selves, Our Souls and Bodies: Sexuality and the Household of God* (Cambridge, MA: Cowley Publications, 1996), in particular the article by Martin L. Smith SSJE, 'Intimate listening: paying attention to the religious experience of gay and lesbian people', pp. 69–75.

50   In the case of a non-Christian something analogous would be presumed such as a religious environment and the hope that the directee would contribute to his/her religious tradition in some way. For an attempt to develop a spirituality of sexuality not dependent on a specifically religious context, see *The Human Core of Spirituality* by Daniel Helminiak (New York: SUNY, 1996), pp. 233–67.

51   For a discussion of direction, counselling and therapy see Chapter 3 of Leech, *Soul Friend*. See also the two chapters in Stone, *Theological Context for Pastoral Caregiving*, Chapter 1, 'The distinctiveness of pastoral care' and Chapter 5, 'Spiritual direction' (New York: The Haworth Pastoral Press, 1996). For an approach to pastoral care of homosexuals which requires the celibate life for the gay person and which implies that the homosexual can change their orientation, see *No-Gay Areas?* by Lance Pierson (Cambridge: Grove Books Ltd, 1997).

2

The right of the gay person to have a spiritual life

After what has been presented in the first chapter, it seems strange to begin the treatment of spiritual direction with gay persons with the need to establish their right to have a spiritual life. Is that not the right of every human being? Does that not follow from being created in the image and likeness of God, which is a central religious insight? Whatever we might use as the starting-point for our Christian (and other religious traditions') anthropology – patristic recapitulation, reformation's grace alone, Catholic sacramentalism, or Rahnerian transcendental Thomism – it seems obvious that each human person is called to union with God and that the path to this union is what is called the spiritual life. To assert the opposite would appear to be equal to blasphemy, a denial of the loving kindness of the creator which is a central theme of both the Hebrew and Christian Scriptures. So why the need to begin with the assertion of this right for the gay person? Because, as Francoise Susset puts it:

> Our sexuality is an indivisible aspect of our humanity. To ask us, regardless of our sexual orientation, to deny and reject our sexuality – who we fantasize about, who we desire, who we fall in love with, who we love – is to ask us to split ourselves away from the most fundamental part of our being, the place which is at the center of our humanity, from which all longing, desire, passion and creativity emerges.[1]

I know of no writer who claims that gays do not have the possibility of a spiritual life. In fact, there is a growing literature on the subject of gay spirituality.[2] In spite of that it is necessary to make a case for the spirituality of gay persons because their spirituality precisely as gay is at least implicitly denied in several ways. Two areas where this right is, if not denied, at least, highly qualified are the positions on homosexuality of the Christian churches and the *de facto* legislation regarding gay/lesbian civil rights. We must examine both of these areas in order to establish the right of the gay person to engage in the spiritual task. To leave this issue unaddressed would mean that anything said about spiritual direction with the gay person would be left under a cloud of ambiguity about their spiritual lives at all. Or the process of spiritual direction would be highly prejudiced in the direction of getting the directees to conform to the positions of the churches or be reduced to helping them to remain in the closet so that they could lessen the amount of discrimination and suffering they would experience in daily life. I suspect that even those who place a negative judgement on homosexuality would be able to see that such is not what is meant by the tradition of spiritual direction as it has been passed on by the religious traditions.

The Christian Churches and Homosexuality

First we turn to the Christian churches because, as noted in the Introduction, the primary audience of this book are Christians.[3] I try to provide here for the director and directee a view of what is happening in the churches in regard to homosexuality that I consider basic for their interaction.[4] The treatment is far from exhaustive. As has already been pointed out, this is not a book on ethics, nor one on moral theology. The intention is not to present the full position of any denomination regarding the morality of homosexuality. That has been more than adequately taken care of by other sources, to some of which I will be referring.[5] The topic of this book is spiritual direction with gay persons, especially as it is experienced in the Christian denominations. The concern is with spirituality. Certainly, there is a connection between the ethical life and the spiritual life, but they are not synonymous.[6] One cannot be reduced to the other. Unhappily, such was the case for Roman Catholic seminarians in much of their seminary training between the Council of Trent and the Second Vatican Council.

There was something in traditional Catholic theology that went by the vague title of mystical theology, but what often passed for spirituality was little more than moral theology coated in more personalistic terms to make it more palatable. Few would maintain that this is what spirituality is today. Now Christian spirituality has established itself as an experience in its own right and so worthy to be studied as a separate discipline.[7] Happily, this interest in spirituality now has moved well beyond the confines of Roman Catholicism. It was during the late 1960s and 1970s when I was participating in the life of several Protestant seminaries in Berkeley, California, that I experienced the reawakening of interest in spirituality and spiritual direction among Protestant seminarians.[8] Because spirituality is an ecumenical concern, directors need to be aware of the varying discussions taking place in all the Christian churches regarding homosexuality.[9]

Caught in the Crossfire: Helping Christians Debate Homosexuality[10] attempts to give both sides of the argument regarding Christian gays/ lesbians. If we keep in mind that each denomination has its own particular emphasis in this matter,[11] this book represents in general the discussion going on in the churches. Pairs of authors, one conservative, the other liberal,[12] address several topics such as: what does the Bible say about homosexuality? what does science teach about homosexuality? are Christianity and homosexuality incompatible? and so on. Using the imagery of weaving, Donald Messer does a concluding chapter on a theology of homosexuality in which he summarizes the two positions on homosexuality under the warp threads of Scripture, tradition, experience, reason and the weft threads of God the creator, human nature and sin, grace and Jesus Christ, and Church and ministry. He shows how differently each side treats each of the threads. Sometimes the difference is radical, sometimes subtle. Here are some excerpts from the thread, God as creator:

> *Probably the foremost and most fundamental question posed is whether being gay or lesbian is a matter of choice or a mode of creation* . . . Conservatives who speak of homosexuality as 'unnatural' or 'contrary to God's intended plan' believe people were not created that way by God. Or they view homosexuality as a 'flaw' in creation or a sinful result of 'the Fall' that needs repentance and correction. Generally, persons who affirm traditional views reject theories that advocate a genetic or constitutional basis for homosexuality.[13]

Messer points out that the liberal side would see same-sex relationships in the context of a God who allows for variation in creation, that the stories of creation as found in the Hebrew Scriptures are not scientific explanations but are literary expressions. Jesus himself said nothing about homosexuality, and condemnation of homosexuals seems inconsistent with his gospel of love. Homosexuality, whether due to genetic causes or to socialization, is, like all sexuality, a gift from God.[14]

The conservatives stress the various scriptural references that condemn homosexual practices while the liberal side emphasizes the area of social sin and how gays/lesbians are not only sinners but those who are sinned against by society and individuals. The history of the Christian Church is chequered when it comes to the point of gay-bashing and the physical and psychological violence perpetrated against persons of this orientation. If homosexuality is a sin, then is not being homophobic also sinful?[15]

Part of the debate is whether homosexuals can and should change. The conservatives tend to be more optimistic about this while the liberals point to the evidence that would support that such orientation is lifelong and that attempts to change it have been more unsuccessful than successful. For conservatives, gays and lesbians must pledge themselves to a life of celibacy, while liberals emphasize that celibacy is a gift chosen freely, not imposed upon people by a God who created them that way in the first place.[16]

For those for whom homosexual practice is but proof of the fall and human depravity, Jesus is the one who comes preaching repentance and who will judge us on the last day. Grace is not cheap. The gate to salvation is narrow. These are all familiar themes that have been part of the Christian tradition. But for those who do not see all homosexual practices as sinful, the picture of Jesus is one who calls everyone to his kingdom, who is always welcoming to all people, especially to the marginalized and oppressed. Jesus does not ask us to reject our sexuality but that we exercise it in a responsible and loving fashion. The commandment 'Love one another as I have loved you' should be the guiding norm for human relationships, not a small section of the book of Leviticus.[17]

For conservatives the Bible is clear and simple: sex is heterosexual, restricted to monogamous marriage and allowed nowhere else. Liberals think this is too simplistic to describe a biblical sexual ethic. Conservatives claim they do not hate gays and lesbians. It is a matter of loving the sinner but hating the sin.[18]

When discussing Church and ministry Messer admits that here especially the labels of conservative and liberal break down the most. The same people take a conservative position on some issues but not on others; liberals are liberal on some points but not others. He summarizes this way:

> Generally, the more 'liberal' or 'mainline' denominations have supported the civil rights of gays and lesbians, while more 'conservative' or evangelical churches have been less public in their support or worked in clear opposition to efforts to ensure homosexual rights or to remove sodomy laws.[19]

And even those who support civil rights for gays/lesbians do not necessarily do the same regarding rights in the Church, such as ordination to the ministry. However, what are we to make of the fact that at certain times in the history of the Church it was not so antagonistic to gays/lesbians and that then and now many members of the Church's ordained ministry were and are gay?[20] Both sides see the Church as a community of compassion but while one side notes the lack of solidarity with those suffering because of their sexual orientation, the other side stresses that love of the homosexual does not entail approval of their practices. Messer notes that a future battleground for the churches will be same-sex unions. In fact, that conflict has already surfaced in the recent court decision in Hawaii which says that for the state to disallow these unions may be unconstitutional.[21]

Messer concludes with a call to disagree in love. That may be important for a general mode of procedure in the churches at any time, but in the area of spiritual direction we need to be more conclusive. Many others who, like myself, have worked in spiritual direction with gays and lesbians would find elements on both sides of the debate with which we would agree or disagree on the basis of our own extensive experience in direction. I suspect that the majority of us would find more on the liberal side than on the conservative side that we could affirm. An important reason for this is that the conservative argument tends to be scripturally literalistic or insufficiently nuanced. When dealing with people's spiritual lives we are rarely dealing with something which can simply be categorized in black and white terms. Also, the emphasis in the conservative argument moves more along ethical and moralistic lines than specifically spiritual ones.[22] Christianity is not an ethical system articulated primarily in terms of moral imperatives. Certainly, Christianity has concrete moral implications, but it is primarily a tradition of a worshipping community which expresses its relationship to God, its spirituality, in terms of symbols, metaphors, images and ascetical practices.[23] The very nature of a symbol is that it is multi-dimensional, not given to easy categorization. The spiritual life is a symbolic life, a sacramental life, the greater part of which lies in the area of the unconscious, and not, as many believe, on the conscious plane or level of the conscience.

The study by the World Council of Churches

In order to examine in more detail the issues regarding homosexuality and the churches I present here some observations regarding the study done by the staff of the World Council of Churches which saw the need to address the issue of homosexuality in the ecumenical context. This led to three staff workshops facilitated by Alan A. Brash, a former deputy general of the WCC. Out of these workshops grew a WCC publication called *Facing Our Differences: The Churches and Their Gay and Lesbian Members*.[24] Brash, a presbyterian minister from New Zealand, begins with his personal story of coming to awareness of the issues of homo-sexuality rather late in life. He notes that up to the present time no extensive discussion of homosexuality has taken place within inter-national ecumenical circles. *Facing Our Differences* is a brief, clear and adequate summary of the debate going on in the churches. Brash begins with some clarifications regarding sexuality itself. The concluding paragraph of his chapter on sexuality is one to which most Christians would readily ascribe and certainly one that most directors would find to be basic in the practice of spiritual direction with gays or straights:

> Sexuality is an aspect of the whole person, which expresses itself in many ways, of which genital activity is only one. Sexuality is part of our whole personality, and our whole personality is involved in its expression. A useful comparison is verbal communication: when we speak, it is not only our lips and vocal cords that are involved but our whole being; when we write, it is not only the work of our fingers but the communication of our whole person. Sexuality is also the expression of our whole selves, and as such it a great, good and enriching gift of God our creator.[25]

It would seem impossible to engage in fruitful dialogue with anyone with whom we cannot have this statement as our common ground. This includes the director and the directee and only when it is accepted by the directee does advancement in the spiritual life seem a realistic possibility.

As noted in the first chapter, I am uncomfortable making a clear-cut distinction between spiritual direction and psychological therapy. They are not the same but neither are they easily distinguishable.[26] Becoming holy and becoming more fully human is more of a mental distinction than one which can be found in the world outside our minds. Nevertheless, this does not imply that spiritual direction has fulfilled its mission once it has made someone comfortable with their sexuality, no matter the fashion in which it is practised. Religious commitment will almost always be an issue in spiritual direction. That means that at some stage in the direction the director and directee will need to deal with the directee's thoughts and feelings about his/her church's stance toward homosexuality.[27]

Brash is primarily concerned with the churches of the Anglican and Protestant traditions. He admits the diversity which is found among these churches regarding the presence of gays and lesbians. He refers to some of the work of the Anglican Church which might be used as a form of generalization regarding the debate in the churches. This would include the Roman Catholic Church because, although the official position is clearly and forcefully stated, there is little evidence that the discussion among Roman Catholics is now at an end.[28] In November 1987 the General Synod of the Church of England voted for four affirmations regarding sexuality, the third of which is pertinent here:

> That homosexual genital acts also fall short of this ideal, (total commitment in marriage) and are likewise to be met by a call to repentance and the exercise of compassion.[29]

This affirmation was not well received and further discussions led to another report that the homosexual orientation and its expression is not an alternative form of sexuality. It falls short of the completeness of heterosexual sexuality. But those who believe that they are called to the same-sex partnership lifestyle are not to be condemned and should not be barred from ordination unless they are sexually active.[30] The conversation in each of the churches would be a variation on this main theme but the general picture is one where increasingly the orientation is seen in a less negative light. In some churches it is granted equal spiritual status with heterosexuality, but the dividing lines comes in the area of genital acts. Clearly, for some churches the official position still refuses to accept same-sex genital acts as activity which can be integrated into gospel values.[31] Others seem to be more accepting of these acts, at least, implicitly, if their ministers do not practise them.

What is valuable about these discussions and of particular significance for the gay persons who want their call to holiness to be validated by religious institutions is the clarification that is taking place. Misunderstandings are being cleared up so that they cannot be used as arguments against the right of gays to pursue their relationship with God in terms of their own sexuality. Let us look at one example of a misunderstanding. Brash briefly summarizes present scholarship which holds that the sin of Sodom is not anal intercourse between two men but rather a form of rape.

> To use the word 'Sodom' or any of its derivatives to refer to any form of sexual intimacy other than rape by anal intercourse not only misrepresents this ancient story but also ignores the meaning given to this ancient city by Jesus and so many of the great prophets of Israel. All of them refer to Sodom as the symbol for punishment for a great variety of sins, but none of them refers to sexual sins.[32]

The sin of Sodom is but one example of how ecumenical discussions and debate in the churches informed by scriptural scholarship is freeing gays and lesbians from the narrowness of biblical interpretation which in the past has blocked their integration into their religious communities. In a further chapter we shall deal with the place of Scripture in the spirituality of gays, but for now it is important to keep in mind Brash's observation that the debates in the churches have focused on the interpretation of relatively few biblical texts, especially those from Leviticus and the epistles of Paul. 'But it is important to note that restricting the discussion of the biblical testimony to these particular texts ignores that part of the scriptural message to which gay and lesbian people refer when they are speaking of themselves.'[33] This restrictiveness has ignored the deeper sense of Scripture which embodies Jesus's concern for the marginated, the poor, the suffering and all those in need of liberation.

The growing scholarship on homosexuality on the part of religious thinkers and theologians, as well as anthropologists, psychologists and historians is bringing about a reconsideration of our understanding of the historical dimension. The story of how the Judaeo-Christian tradition has itself been one of the worst examples of the oppression of gays and lesbians has been told and detailed elsewhere.[34] And within the Christian Church itself the practice and official teaching have not always gone together. Research is continuing to surface evidence that the spirit of compassion and the ethic of love of Jesus triumphed over theological positions in the daily lives of people. A good example of such research would be John Boswell's *Same Sex Unions in Pre-Modern Europe*[35] where he presents the evidence for liturgies for uniting two people of the same sex. Brash sums up succinctly our reflections on the history of same-sex relationships when he says:

> [It] is sufficient to indicate the radical change in understanding that results when it is recognized that for some people the desire for such relationships is innate and unchangeable, and in no way an act of choice for which they can be held responsible . . . In earlier centuries, people were unaware of that fact.[36]

Although this may explain the treatment of gays and lesbians in the past, it cannot be used for the continuance of such treatment. Change has been taking place. Clearly, it would be naive to presume that the days of discrimination and suffering are over for gays. Still there seems to be a gradual lifting of the burden from the shoulders of gays and lesbians. It is another stone removed away from the tomb (closet?) in which the past has tried to bury them.[37]

Homosexuality and pastoral care[38]

In 1982 the Commission on Social Justice of the Archdiocese of San Francisco put out an elaborate report on the issue.[39] Chapter Five of the Report, 'Spiritual Lives of Lesbian Woman and Gay Men', clearly states the problem about which this chapter is concerned:

> It seems to come as a surprise to some people that lesbian women and gay men have spiritual lives at all. Generally accepted myths

regarding spirituality and the homosexual person involve mis-perceptions such that God is not with and among gay men and lesbian women, that lesbian women and gay men do not seek God in their lives, or that their spirituality is largely focused on and filtered through a syndrome of moments of weakness, struggles for a firm purpose of amendment, and a search for understanding confessors who will administer the sacrament of Penance and Eucharist as spiritual aids for a firmer resolve towards venereal abstinence.[40]

Spiritual directors of Christians, and perhaps Roman Catholics in particular, will recognize that such has been the experience in the majority of their gay directees. Few of these people will have experienced their admission to the spiritual life except in a kind of begrudging way. It is a spiritual life in spite of who they are. Most will not have been encouraged to grow in intimacy with others precisely as gay persons with gay feelings and gay inclinations. And unless the directee has been in direction with other directors, they probably will not have been encouraged to enjoy being gay, to be proud of being gay, to rejoice in being gay.

The Report points out the distinction between lesbian women and gay men that is often part of the experience. Lesbians labour under the double oppression of being both homosexual and being women. The Catholic lesbian will feel unwelcome on many counts: sexism, homo-phobia, the legitimation of male superiority in society, and theology and church doctrine which has been based on male experience. In working with these lesbians it is especially important for the director to be aware of the sources of liberation for these women: liberation theology, the feminist perspectives, and certain contemporary theological develop-ments such as a theology of friendship.[41]

The Report also pointed out that the gays and lesbians that were interviewed did not see their spiritual lives only in the negative terms noted above. There were also those for whom their sexuality was more a gift than a wound. Their lives often were in a movement between oppression and celebration. One man, a Roman Catholic, spoke of the intense pain he has experienced in being Roman Catholic and a homosexual. For him it is the great irony that the institution, which could help eliminate some of the societal injustice to gays, actually perpetrates it even more, in some instances, allowing for the possible violence against and contempt for the dignity of the homosexual person.[42] He speaks of the great dilemma for lesbian women and gay men in the Church when the Church defends the supremacy of their conscience but condemns their activity as objectively sinful. His final painful but poignant statement will be one that most directors of church-going gays will instantly recognize:

> I suppose, after all is said and done, that I could fulfill my destiny with God without the Church, and many times I have left her, but always to find myself coming back. I cannot desert her, for she is the only mother I have. Where else am I to go? I cry at her doorstep, and when she does not hear, I pound on her doors, for I am her son, and I am lonely and I need her comfort.[43]

The Report, although issued some years ago, is still correct in stating the dilemma for the gay person wishing to pursue a spiritual life. Since the Report was published there have been an increasing number of statements from the churches encouraging a ministry to gays/lesbians. Usually these statements recognize the legitimate needs of these people, accept the fact of discrimination in the churches against them in the past, call for a discarding of distorted pictures of them, and exhort the churches to listen to their gay and lesbian brothers and sisters for what they can offer to the rest of us. But almost all these statements also make the distinction between orientation and behaviour and urge the celibate life on homosexuals. The Report, on the other hand, found that few of the people they interviewed saw the celibate life as their calling and that their active sexual lives were for them experienced as good and their way to God.[44]

Anyone doing direction with the gay person will meet in the course of their work many gays such as those described in this Report: mature, committed men and women who are active in their churches, and whose lives are of the highest integrity. And although some of us directors might judge their sexual activity as falling short of the Christian ideal, the rest of their lives would not come under the same judgement.[45] Honesty demands that we acknowledge that at times the degree of courage displayed by gay men and women in their search for God in an ambiguous situation is impressive. In fact, it is their particular form of marginalization which seems to give them some particular insights into the journey to God and the experience of the sacred in the world today. I detail this in the chapters which follow.

The Report gives the statements of two spiritual directors working with gays and lesbians in trying to answer the question: is there a spirituality that is unique for gay men and lesbian women? One director says that there is. In this director's words: 'That uniqueness is based on two factors contained in the life experience of lesbian women and gay men: first, coping with the *loss of expectations*, and second, *the "coming out" process*.'[46] There is a real loss in the lives of gays and that is the expectation of being heterosexual. It is a loss on their part because they perceive their difference from other males and females, usually rather early in life, and they experience the loss of expectations on the part of family and friends. Unless the loss is accepted and mourned, it will be difficult to move ahead in the spiritual life in a positive way. Also, this spiritual director sees the coming-out process for gays and lesbians as similar to the process of individuation that Carl Jung describes. This is the search for the true self by letting go of ego, by confronting one's shadow, and by integrating the anima in one's life. This journey is a difficult one and that is why spiritual direction is important at this time. Any direction must take into account these two sources of spiritual growth, helping the person to deal with the loss of expectations and facilitating the coming-out process. Direction should help all directees in the uniqueness of their journey and certainly the journey of the gay man has its own kind of uniqueness.[47] I deal with the two areas of loss of expectations and the coming-out process explicitly in the last three chapters of the book which focus on the stages of adult development.

Homosexuality and social justice

If the first cause of the denial (often implicit) of the right of gays to have a spiritual life has been due to the ambiguity of the Christian churches towards them in terms of the morality of their actions, the second surely is located in the matter of social justice, including civil rights.[48] Probably the instance which most highlights the conflict in the area of social justice for Roman Catholic gays and lesbians is the statement issued by the Vatican's Congregation for the Doctrine of the Faith, 'Some Considerations Concerning the Catholic Response to Legislative Proposals on the Non-Discrimination of Homosexual Persons'.[49] Richard Peddicord OP, in an excellent study called *Gay and Lesbian Rights: A Question: Social Ethics or Social Justice?*,[50] says about this document:

The cornerstone of this document is that insistence that there are times when society *ought* to discriminate against homosexual persons. When gay people attempt employment which would put them in close contact with children or when they try to adopt children, they should be opposed. Moreover, as a rule of thumb, the civil rights of gays and lesbians are dependent upon their remaining invisible to society at large. For SCC (this document), the Church's negative moral evaluation of 'homosexual acts' is the principle from which all else flows.[51]

Peddicord goes on to argue in favour of the civil rights of gays/lesbians by moving away from the perspective of Catholic sexual ethics being the determining factor in justifying such discrimination. Rather, if we begin with Catholic social teaching which emphasizes human dignity, human rights, the importance of conscience, and respect for those who follow their conscience, then this perspective supports laws against all forms of discrimination including discrimination against gays and lesbians.[52]

Such statements as the one coming from the Congregation for the Doctrine of the Faith tend to reinforce the attitudes the director finds in many of the directees: lack of self-affirmation, poor self-image, an abiding sense of guilt, and constant questioning about their relationship with the Church, if not with God. Such a public position can only make many Catholics wonder whatever happened to the loving Christ of the New Testament, when what is supposed to be his Body in the present world can speak in a way so divergent from its very own proclamation of the good news. It comes across as bad news for many Catholics and makes it difficult for them to hear the good news which may be there. And not only Catholics, but all Christians, are affected by such a statement. It is a public declaration which only heightens for them the ambiguity they find in their own churches.

By employing the work of the theologian John Courtney Murray on the relationship of Church and State, Peddicord argues persuasively that 'support for gay and lesbian rights legislation and (or) municipal ordinances is well within the parameters of Catholic moral teaching'.[53] He concludes his significant work with these words:

It is inconsistent for members of the American Catholic hierarchy to call for justice for gay people and then attempt to block the legislation which would serve to ensure this justice. Opposing the morality of certain sexual practices ought not to entail collusion with campaigns to place social and economic obstacles in the path of an already undervalued social minority.[54]

Vincent J. Genovesi SJ, in his article on the social implications of homosexuality, gives the best summary statement regarding the civil rights of gays and lesbians that I have found anywhere. He says there is something invidious about claims that gay-rights legislation is not necessary if gays keep their sexual orientation to themselves, that is, remain chastely in the closet. Genovesi challenges this way of thinking so articulately that it deserves a full quotation.

> Are homosexuals truly safe, or even free, in their secretiveness when they must always live with the fear of being discovered? And even if this were a safe way to live, we must ask if it is a healthy way to live humanly, psychologically, and spiritually. And is it not itself a form of oppression to require as the price to be paid for the exercise of their civil rights that gays and lesbians live in silent deceit, pretending to be other than they truly are? Having to live in such a way would seem to be demeaning and debilitating to homosexuals themselves, and it certainly does nothing to challenge others in society to greater moral sensitivity and maturity. In fact, advising homosexuals to remain invisible only reinforces the vicious circle in which society is trapped; when homosexuals surrender to society's general intolerance by remaining invisible, they effectively allow the stereotypical images by which they are portrayed to go unchallenged; in turn, these images feed the very homophobia that results in the intolerance and discrimination that already make so many homosexuals' invisibility necessary or expedient.[55]

Concluding remark

It will not be the case that every gay man or woman seeking spiritual direction will need to be reassured that they can have a spiritual life precisely as a gay person. But there will be many who will. It will be the director's task to be honest about the issues discussed in this chapter: the mixed positions of the churches and the lack of social justice both in the Church and civil society. The gay Christian in spiritual direction will most likely be an active participant in church life. And, obviously, there is no way they can avoid being part of society. While being honest about the various church positions and problems caused by discrimination, the director will often find that s/he needs to nuance church teaching to avoid it being manipulated for destructive purposes and to stress that society's discriminatory practices are based on the sin of others and not that of the gay person. It is hoped that the following chapters will assist the director and the directee to strengthen their conviction that the call to the spiritual life comes from God and that no church or society can take that right away. In the words of Joseph H. Neisen:

> Numerous traditional religious institutions have tried to convince lesbians and gays that it is not possible for us to embrace spirituality because of our sexual orientation. On the contrary, our sexual orientation and the religious abuse we have suffered have propelled us to examine our spirituality in much more depth than many heterosexuals can ever hope to.
>
> Ours is not a spirituality that is measured by the number of times we attend a church service. Instead, it is a deep personal examination about the meaning of life, our role in life, how our gayness can be celebrated and how our gifts can be shared rather than stifled.
>
> Being gay does not preclude spirituality. Openly embracing one's gayness is a form of spirituality.[56]

Notes

1   Joseph H. Neisen, *Reclaiming Pride: Daily Reflections on Gay and Lesbian Life* (Deerfield Beach, FL: Health Communications, 1994), p. ix.

2   This literature is still small, as is that pertaining to gay theology. Some of the books on gay theology hardly merit the title of theology. This is in contrast to feminist theology and feminist spirituality, which now refers to a formidable body of writings and equally formidable scholars. The hope is that gay spirituality and gay theology will one day achieve the recognition and quality that now characterizes the feminist critique. The makings of a gay spirituality is found in books which deal with homosexuality and religion such as Brian Bouldrey (ed.), *Wrestling with the Angel* (New York: Riverhead Books, 1995). But these tend to be anecdotal and pastoral in character. We still await a consistently developed approach that moves beyond the emphasis of this present chapter. However, in the meantime, good books to be familiar with include, Andre Guidon, *The Sexual Creators: An Ethical Proposal for Concerned Christians* (New York: University Press of America, 1986). See Chapter 7: 'Gay fecundity or liberating sexuality', for contributions to the world that gay men make.

3 There are now available many publications which give the positions of the churches with the attendant discussions taking place. Those seeking a brief, matter-of-fact description of the situation of homosexuality in the Catholic Church would find it helpful to read the chapter on homosexuality in Thomas C. Fox, *Sexuality and Catholicism* (New York: George Braziller, 1995). A very good reference book here is Jeannine Gramick and Robert Nugent (eds), *Voices of Hope: A Collection of Positive Catholic Writings on Gay and Lesbian Issues* (New York: Center for Homophobia Education, 1995). The editors have excerpted texts from larger works to provide a resource for those looking for positive and informed statements on homosexuality in a Catholic context. The voices that speak here are not the harsh and insensitive ones. This volume contains brief statements on civil rights and pastoral care for gays/lesbians from Catholic leaders from 1973 to 1995, such writings as various diocesan plans and pastoral letters, and responses to the 1992 Vatican document on non-discrimination against gays and lesbians. The statement by Cardinal Joseph Bernadin is a good example of how many ecclesiastical leaders find themselves caught in upholding the teaching of the Catholic Church and their desire for pastoral care for gays and lesbians. Bernadin's statement (pp. 219ff.) is a clarion call for gay rights and a clear condemnation of discriminatory practices against homosexuals. The dilemma is when he limits intimate sexual relations to heterosexual marriage. He says:

> I realize that, when I say this, I upset many who are gay and lesbian. They do not understand how I can support fundamental human rights and at the same time not endorse homosexual activity. Some, in fact, become quite angry and accuse me of being duplicitous. To their anger I can only respond with love and ask that, as I respect them, could they not respect me and my belief?

4 For a brief but comprehensive and well-balanced discussion of the debate regarding homosexuality from a particularly British point of view see David Leal, *Debating Homosexuality* (Cambridge: Grove Books, 1996).

5 For the views of the Christian churches see J. Gordon Melton, *The Churches Speak on Homosexuality: Official Statements from Religious Bodies and Ecumenical Organizations* (Detroit: Galre Research, 1991).

6 For a balanced attempt from a mainly Protestant perspective to develop an ethic as a response to the issues surrounding homosexuality see Kathy Rudy, *Sex and the Church: Gender, Homosexuality, and the Transformation of Christian Ethics* (Boston: Beacon Press, 1997).

7 One need only take note of two important organizations and their publications to become convinced that ethics is not the same as spirituality: The Society for the Study of Christian Spirituality and its journal, *Christian Spirituality Bulletin* and Spiritual Directors International and its publication, *Presence*.

8 Often the Protestant seminarians would come to spiritual direction to the Catholic professors because those of their own tradition were not comfortable taking on that role.

9 In 1994 *The Other Side* magazine published a special issue, 'Christian and homosexuality: dancing toward the light' (300 W. Apsley St, Philadelphia, Pa. 19144). The articles take a very positive view of gays and lesbians and their rights in

society. What is interesting is that this is a periodical which has evangelical roots and that it is speaking out for gay and lesbian Christians.

10 Sally B. Geis and Donald E. Messer (eds), *Caught in the Crossfire: Helping Christians Debate Homosexuality* (Nashville: Abingdon Press, 1994).

11 Leanne McCall Tigert, *Coming Out While Staying In* (Cleveland: United Church Press, 1996), surveys the issue of homophobia in the mainline churches from the perspective of a United Church of Christ minister. She brings a psychological dimension to her theological reflections. In an appendix she includes 'Welcoming congregation statements from several denominations' and 'UCC pronouncements and resolutions regarding lesbian/gay/bisexual concerns'.

12 I am fully aware of the limitations of using such labels as 'conservative' and 'liberal', but they are the ones used by Messer. I believe there is enough truth in what these labels refer to that I am justified in using them also.

13 Geis and Messer, *Caught in the Crossfire*, p. 177.

14 Geis and Messer, *Caught in the Crossfire*, p. 178. Dean Hamer and Peter Copeland, *The Science Of Desire: The Search for the Gay Gene and the Biology of Behavior* (New York: Simon and Schuster, 1994), is a study of Dean Hamer's work on a genetic link making homosexuality inheritable. Although Hamer and his colleagues have not yet discovered the gay gene, their discussion of the various issues of genetic manipulation and their rejection of 'nature versus nurture' can be enlightening for those in spiritual direction. A genetic link does not mean everyone with the gene will be gay or that all gays have a gay gene.

15 Geis and Messer, *Caught in the Crossfire*, pp. 180–1.

16 Geis and Messer, *Caught in the Crossfire*, pp. 181–2.

17 The relationship of the love of God and the love of neighbour is found throughout the New Testament. The great commandment and the second one after it are found in Mark 12:31; Matt. 22:29; Rom. 13:8ff. and Gal. 5:14. The two commandments cannot be separated (1 John 4:20ff.). For a detailed discussion of the meaning of love in the Bible see the article, 'Love', in Alan Richardson (ed.), *A Theological WordBook of the Bible* (New York: Macmillan, 1960), pp. 131–6. See also John L. McKenzie SJ, *Dictionary of the Bible* (Milwaukee: The Bruce Publishing Company, 1965).

18 Geis and Messer, *Caught in the Crossfire*, pp. 183–5.

19 Geis and Messer, *Caught in the Crossfire*, p. 186.

20 See John Boswell, *Christianity Social Tolerance and Homosexuality* (Chicago: University of Chicago Press, 1980).

21 Geis and Messer, *Caught in the Crossfire*, p. 187. An intelligent discussion of the Hawaiian case is found in *The Advocate* (4 February 1997), pp. 22ff. The case has not yet been finally resolved. For a follow-up on the case see *The Advocate* (27 May 1997), p. 71. Although homosexual couples in Hawaii cannot marry, they have won reciprocal over-60 benefits. The reaction in many states to the possibility of same-sex marriages means that those promoting the rights of gays to get married have a difficult battle ahead. There are clear differences among the Christian denominations in the United States. For instance, *The New York Times* (22 July 1997) reported that the chapel at Harvard University is now open to having commitment or blessing ceremonies for lay and lesbian couples. In the same article

it quotes the policy of the United Methodist Church: 'Ceremonies that celebrate homosexual unions shall not be conducted by our ministers and shall not be conducted in our churches.' More discussion about gay marriages is found in *The Harvard Gay and Lesbian Review* (Fall 1997). See Andrew Sullivan, 'Marriage is a basic civil right' (pp. 25–8) and Chai Feldblum, 'Keep the sex in same-sex marriage' (pp. 23–5). For a comprehensive and scholarly presentation of same-sex unions there is no better work than John Boswell, *Same-sex Unions in PreModern Europe* (New York: Vintage Books, 1994).

22 It was pointed out to me that a consideration of the Holy Spirit in the spiritual journey is lacking in the conservative approach to this issue.

23 As spiritual direction moves into the more advanced stages, it will take on more a spirit of worship than of counselling, problem solving or moral theology.

24 Alan A. Brash, *Facing Our Differences: The Churches and Their Gay and Lesbian Members*, Risk Book Series (Geneva; WCC Publications, 1995).

25 *Ibid.*, p. 16.

26 It all depends on the therapist and the director in the concrete. Even the distinction noted earlier, that in therapy I lie down on a couch and pay a fee, has been blurred. Payment is frequently part of the direction practice (although usually not as much as therapy) and we could lie down during direction if we so desired. In fact, many spiritual masters of the past, such as Ignatius of Loyola, recommend various positions for prayer, one of which is lying on the floor.

27 As already noted, the focus in direction will be on the actual feelings, thoughts, and judgements of the directee rather than the morality of his/her position. The latter is the more appropriate matter for confession (in those denominations which have the practice of confession).

28 For a comprehensive study of gays and lesbians in the Catholic Church see Robert Nugent and Jeannine Gramick, *Building Bridges: Gay and Lesbian Reality and the Catholic Church* (Mystic, CT: Twenty-Third Publications, 1992). They examine the experience of Roman Catholic homosexuals from four viewpoints: educational and social concerns, counselling and pastoral issues, religious and clerical life, and evolving theological perspectives. See Jack A. Bonsor, 'An objective disorder: homosexual orientation and God's eternal law', *Horizons*, **24** (2) (Fall 1997), pp. 193–214. Bonsor re-examines the Thomistic understanding of natural law and in light of this examination calls for a rethinking of the Catholic Church's position on homosexuality.

29 See Brash, *Facing Our Differences*, p. 25.

30 *Ibid.*, p. 26. The Lambeth Conference of 1998, a meeting of the bishops of the worldwide Anglican Communion, endorsed a resolution that declared that homosexual activity is incompatible with Scripture and that homosexuals should best not be ordained (reported in the *New York Times*, 6 August 1998).

31 This is the position of the Roman Catholic Church. For instance, *The Catechism of the Catholic Church* (London: Geoffrey Chapman, 1994), when it refers to homosexual acts as being contrary to natural law, says: 'Under no circumstances can they be approved' (2357). The next paragraph (2358) also states: 'The number of men and women who have deep-seated homosexual tendencies is not negligible. They do not choose their homosexual condition; for most of them it is a trial. They

must be accepted with respect, compassion and sensitivity. Every sign of unjust discrimination in their regard is to be avoided.'

32 Brash, *Facing Our Differences*, p. 38.

33 *Ibid.*, p. 46.

34 See Boswell, *Christian Social Tolerance and Homosexuality*. For a study of same-sex love outside the Judaeo-Christian tradition, see Christine Downing's analysis of the experience of homosexuality in ancient Greece in *Myths and Mysteries of Same-Sex Love* (New York: Continuum, 1990).

35 (New York: Villard Press, 1994.) This is the hardcover publication. The Vintage Books edition is in paperback.

36 Brash, *Facing our Differences*, p. 53.

37 For more on the relationship of homosexuality and the Church see: Keith Hartman, *Congregations in Conflict: The Battle over Homosexuality* (New Brunswick, NJ: Rutgers University Press, 1996). This is a series of case studies. It has the value of making very concrete what the author claims in his preface: that homosexuality is the most divisive issue in the Church today, that it stirs up strong emotions, and splits congregations and denominations. It brings up the most basic issues such as how one tells right from wrong, what is the meaning of the Bible and to what extent the Church is doing God's will in the matter. Directors working with gay priests and ministers would find the book helpful. Jeffrey S. Siker, in his *Homosexuality in the Church: Both Sides of the Debate* (Louisville: Westminister/John Knox Press, 1994), has gathered a group of scholars, each of whom make their own contribution to various aspects of homosexuality as it is being discussed in the churches today. An appendix contains statements on homosexuality from various Protestant churches. John J. McNeill in his book, *The Church and the Homosexual* (Kansas City: Sheed Andrews and McMeel, 1976) tried to do by himself what Siker did with several authors, namely, look at the issue of homosexuality and the Church from Scripture, tradition, moral theology, the human sciences and pastoral ministry. Gary David Comstock, *Unrepentant, Self-Affirming, Practicing* (New York: Continuum, 1996), provides a forum for gays and lesbians who are involved within organized religion to give their views about their religious communities. Richard Hasbany (ed.), *Homosexuality and Religion* (New York: Harrington Park Press, 1989), has the advantage of adding the Jewish perspective to that of the Catholic and Protestant. Gareth Moore, *Body in Context* (London: SCM Press, 1992) supports gay people against contemporary Catholic opponents.

38 *Open Hands: Resources for Ministries Affirming the Diversity of Human Sexuality* (3801 N. Keeler Ave., Chicago, IL., 60641) is a quarterly which is a resource for congregations and individuals seeking to be in ministry with lesbian, bisexual and gay persons. Each issue focuses on a specific area of concern within the Church.

39 *Homosexuality and Social Justice: Report of the Task Force on Gay/Lesbian Issues* (San Francisco: Commission on Social Justice, Archdiocese of San Francisco, July 1982).

40 *Ibid.*, p. 73.

41 *Ibid.*, p. 74.

42 This became a public issue at the time of the Cardinal Ratzinger report, which is treated below.

43   *Homosexuality and Social Justice*, p. 79.

44   *Ibid.*, p. 85.

45   And it is their whole lives which must be considered. Celibate chastity cannot be reduced to non-use of one's genitals. Leanne McCall Tigert points out that all people should be considered chaste by an ethics of love. She quotes Norman Pittenger and James Nelson: 'An ethics of love mandates against selfish sexual expression, cruelty, impersonal sex, obsession with sex, and against actions done without willingness to take responsibility for the consequences. Such an ethics always asks about the meanings of acts in their total context – in the relationship itself, in society, and in regard to God's intended direction for human life', *Coming Out While Staying In*, pp. xxi–xxii. Those gays and lesbians who understand that chastity for them also implies a non-genital celibacy may find encouragement in the brief, but positive article, 'Celibacy: the gift of being gay' by Matthew Kelty OCSO, a Cistercian monk of the Abbey of Gethsemani, in 'NURTURING THE GIFT: gay and lesbian persons in seminary and religious formation', *CMI Journal*, **11** (August 1988), pp. 14–16.

46   *Homosexuality and Social Justice*, p. 81.

47   *Ibid.*, pp. 80–3. I am very much in agreement about these two points being significant in the spiritual lives of gays. I would not single them out as the two most important areas that make their spiritual lives unique, but I would not deny their centrality. There is one point about which I am not in agreement with this spiritual director's statement. This director says that the ideal director for the gay and lesbian is a director of the same orientation. I can see some immediate advantages to that. But there is also the danger that the homosexual (like the heterosexual) director could lose objectivity in such a situation. The most important thing about any director is their humanity and how healthy they are as human beings. We must always remember that we are more alike than we are different. Our humanity is more significant to any of us than our sexual orientation. I hope it is obvious by now that in saying this that I am in no way denying the uniqueness of the gay experience. Their vocation rests on the fact that gay people experience the spiritual realities of their lives through their own gay prism. The sense of otherness which propels so many gay men and lesbians to search for transcendence in their lives and to connect with the sacred in their unique way is detailed through a series of anecdotal stories by several gay men in Mark Thompson (ed.), *Gay Soul* (HarperSanFrancisco, 1994).

48   Andrew Sullivan makes the interesting comment that 'Until we have tackled those religious reasons at their core, the political opposition will be impossible to fully dislodge. Until we have fought the theological battle through every scriptural verse and every natural law argument and every liturgical rite, we can forget making real headway in the secular sphere. The battles are distinct, but until we have won one, we will be able to fight the other only to a draw', *The Advocate* (14 October 1997), p. 93. In this article, 'Winning the religious war', Sullivan says that the gay civil rights leadership has ignored religion and so has only ensured its political marginalization. He see this situation changing.

49   See *Origins*, **22** (6 August 1992), pp. 173, 175–7. We should not underestimate the influence that the official Catholic Church statements have on other church-going Christians.

50   Richard Peddicord OP, *Gay and Lesbian Rights: A Question: Social Ethics or Social Justice* (Kansas City: Sheed and Ward, 1996).

51   *Ibid.*, p. ix. For a valuable critique of this document see the article by Vincent Genovesi, 'Social implications of homosexuality', Judith A. Dwyer and Elizabeth L. Montgomery (eds.), *The New Dictionary of Catholic Social Thought* (Collegeville: The Liturgical Press, 1994), pp. 447–53. Genovesi looks at the assumptions which are being made by the statements put out by the Catholic Church as well as society's discriminatory practices regarding such issues as homosexuals in the military and the teaching profession. He sees some advance in the gradual acceptance of domestic partnerships and agrees that the churches need to find some way to support stable homosexual unions. He calls for greater scrutiny of such policies which would forbid gay couples to adopt a child, to have a foster child or have custody of children. He says justice demands that we consider the child and what would be a situation of nurturing love for the child regardless of the sexual orientation of the adopting parents.

52   *Ibid.*, p. ix.

53   *Ibid.*, p. 185. Those who wish to keep abreast of the political news regarding gay and lesbian civil rights might wish to join the Human Rights Campaign. The HRC *Quarterly* contains that kind of information (HRC, 1101 14th St., NW, Suite 200, Washington, D.C. 20005). For instance, the Summer 1997 issue carried articles on the influence of the religious right, the Southern Baptist Convention boycotting of Disney because of its 'gay-friendly' policies, and how the Federal Government moves to address the problem of hate crimes against gays and lesbians. For those interested in studying both sides of the issue of public policy regarding gays, see *Same Sex: Debating the Ethics, Science and Culture of Homosexuality*, ed. John Covino (Oxford: Rowman and Littlefield, 1997). The essays present opposing views regarding issues of morality, identity and history.

54   *Ibid.*, pp. 185–6. William D. Lindsey in his article, 'The AIDS crisis and the Church: a time to heal', in A. Thatcher and E. Stuart (eds), *Christian Perspectives on Sexuality and Gender* (Grand Rapids, MI: Eerdmaus, 1996), pp. 347–66, makes the interesting observation that the American Catholic Church takes a fundamentalist position regarding homosexuality while being more liberal in its social policies. He notes: 'Can the American Catholic Church ally itself with American funda-mentalism without appearing to endorse aspects of the agenda of the Christian Right that are entirely alien to traditional Catholic notions of the good society (e.g. universal health coverage) . . . The Catholic who wishes to promote *all* aspects of Catholic social teaching cannot help being bewildered, since hardly anything in the social and economic views of the American fundamentalist movement reflects the outlook of Catholic social teaching' (p. 359).

55   'Social implications'. Although Richard D. Mohr's book, *A More Perfect Union: Why Straight America Must Stand up for Gay Rights*, is clearly written from an American perspective, it is a good example of how denying rights to gays and lesbians undercuts the rights of all the citizens of a country.

56   Joseph H. Neisen, *Reclaiming Pride: Daily Reflections on Gay and Lesbian Life* (Deerfield Beach, FL: Health Communications, 1994), entry for 22 May.

3

Gay spirituality:
living on the margins

The need for a spiritual life

Everyone needs a spiritual life of some kind if they are to relate to God.
People run the gamut of those who have a well-developed and intentional
spiritual life to those who have never heard of the idea. Those seeking
spiritual guidance will be moving in the direction of the first group.
I would have to rehearse the entire history of spirituality in order
to include all the reasons why it is incumbent upon us to pursue the
spiritual path, the 'journey of the soul to God'. By way of example I want
to consider but one theme, but one which carries with it special import at
this time in human history. This particular experience that many have in
trying to relate to God goes by many names. It is sometimes called the
'dark night of the soul' of John of the Cross. It may be the Kierkegaardian
'dread'.[1] It may be an abiding sense of boredom or even a revulsion
towards what we connected with in the past. Whatever the name, it is an
experience of emptiness, of having lost our way, perhaps, of being
abandoned by God. It is a fear that if we follow the movement towards
God by moving more deeply into ourselves, we will find nothing at all.
For this reason many people do not allow their spiritual direction to go
beyond a certain depth. Therapists have similar experiences.

Probably no one who is serious about the spiritual life is spared this
desert experience, this movement through the night of the senses, this
psychological deprivation, this lack of satisfaction in the good things of
life.[2] I am not suggesting that this is the only or even the most important
issue in spirituality as we move into the twenty-first century. Nor would
I want to reduce the spiritual journey to dealing with this experience. But

it is a pivotal one. This dark night of the soul is probably as pervasive an experience in our spiritual quest as any other concern, such as personal development, dealing with negative self-images, or redoing our images of God.

For many of us it manifests itself in the difficulty with praying. Many find prayer problematic because our scientific, technological society militates against an attitude of dependence, which is necessary in prayer. Prayer presupposes our condition of creaturehood. Many find prayer questionable when confronted with all the evil forces in the world: the power of war, destruction, exclusivity, and the many 'isms' which blind us. It seems that God is either powerless or really does not care. Then, there is the language which we use about God which places God in a special category of distance and unavailability. Many women and men find the masculine-orientated language of God a definite barrier in their attempt to relate to God. All this can constitute an experience of the dark night.

But this experience is also one that can lead us to the very door of divine transcendence. This dark night can steer us toward new experiences as can few other spiritual encounters, except perhaps for the kind St Paul had at his moment of conversion. Only if we consciously develop a spiritual life will we be able to negotiate the passage through this dark night in such a way that we emerge from it better human beings. This is true for all. It is certainly true for gay persons whose dark night is experienced in the context of those who would deny them a right to the spiritual life itself.

The need for a spiritual life does not imply that it can be created on call. In spiritual direction certain issues will present themselves as substitutes for or blocks to spiritual growth. A very common way to inhibit the inner search is to keep ourselves busy about many things. 'The popular notion is that unless people "do" something, they will not "experience" anything – ergo, their frantic activity.'[3] This can mean that we have become strangers to our inner lives, that we feel nothing inside which has not had its source from some external stimulation. It may signal our frustration at not being able to command happiness upon request. Herwig Arts quotes from D. de Rougemont's *Love and the Western World* (p. 265): 'Every wish to experience happiness, to have it at one's beck and call – instead of *being in* a state of happiness as though by grace – must instantly produce an intolerable sense of want.'[4] The spiritual life is not something we possess, something that we produce instantly; it is given to us when we long for God and move to open ourselves to God. This implies that the task on our side is to become a better human being, more fully engaged in the process of expanding our humanity, someone who *can long* for God. God's task is to transform our human journey into the spiritual journey as such. As Gregory Baum said many years ago, it is the humanization process which is salvational. It is possible to give a description of the redemptive presence of God in human life in ordinary language because God is really working everywhere. And the emphasis is on *everywhere* in human life.[5] Spiritual direction is as much about becoming a more fully appropriated person as it is about being in union with God. This humanization process is another way of describing the spiritual life itself. It is also what theologian, Bernard Lonergan, has called 'self-transcendence', or the expansion of the 'horizons' of our being. David Tracy puts it this way:

> One lives authentically insofar as one continues to allow oneself an expanding horizon. This expansion has as its chief aim the going-beyond one's present state in accordance with the transcendental imperatives: be attentive, be intelligent, be reasonable, be responsible, develop and if necessary, change . . . We understand this self-transcending possibility best when we reflect upon our ability to ask questions.[6]

Tracy is referring to what he calls 'limit' experiences. Marginalization and suffering certainly qualify as limit experiences. Spiritual directors will quickly recognize these limit experiences of their gay directees. Much of spiritual direction will be assisting the person in discovering the religious character of these limit experiences. Tracy discusses the limit situations in the world of everyday life. He says:

> All genuine limit-situations refer to those experiences, both positive and negative, wherein we both experience our own human limits (limit-to) as our own as well as recognize, however haltingly, some disclosure of a limit-of our experience.[7]

Limit as an experience of transcendence

The limits we have in our lives are both negative and positive. As negative they include guilt, anxiety, death, illness and in the case of gays the discrimination and oppression they experience in all its forms. These are the times when we may find ourselves impeded from contact with God, family and friends and devoid of meaning. There are also positive limit experiences, those heightened moments of the spiritual in our lives. Love, joy, creativity are all positive limit experiences. These are times when we relish the sense of fulfilment and meaningfulness that overtakes us. They lead us beyond ourselves, and over and above ourselves. But we also experience limit in these situations too. We may be luxuriating in an aesthetic moment or rejoicing in the victory of overcoming a personal crisis, but we also experience our limitation in those very moments. Negative limits for gay men and women mean facing the world with 'a starkness we cannot shirk and manages to disclose to us our basic existential faith or unfaith in life's very meaninglessness'.[8] Gays and lesbians find their positive limits in peak experiences such as moments of coming out, fully embodied love, honesty in the work place, and being with suffering and dying gay brothers and sisters. Referring to those situations, Tracy says:

> When in the grasp of such experiences, we all find, however momentarily, that we can and do transcend our usual lackluster selves and our usual everyday worlds to touch upon a dimension of experience which cannot be stated adequately in the language of ordinary, everyday experience. Authentic love, both erotic and agapic, puts us in touch with a reality whose power we cannot deny . . . In all such authentic moments of ecstasy, we experience a reality simply given, gifted, happened.[9]

One of the purposes of direction is to help the gay person to recognize those times, negative and positive, as truly religious, real experiences of God, fully human and fully Christian. God is really touching them. And for those gays who come to direction but are not connected to the Christian or even any particular religious tradition, it will be this approach to the suffering and marginalization in their lives that will make the most sense to them and make it possible for them to continue their journeys as they move through these limit experiences.

Impasse in the gay man's spiritual life

Constance FitzGerald is someone who has combined the thinking of John of the Cross and his notion of the dark night of the soul with the limit experiences described by David Tracy. Although she is not writing directly to a gay audience, what she has to say can be of enormous benefit for the gay person in direction. She describes the dark night as an impasse, not only a personal one but one which is the dark night of the world. Her description of impasse depicts incredibly well the experience of a gay man or woman coming to spiritual direction for the first time or at an early stage of development.

> By impasse I mean that there is no way out of, no way around, no rational escape from, what imprisons one, no possibilities in the situation. In a true impasse, every normal manner of acting is brought to a standstill, and ironically, impasse is experienced not only in the problem itself but also in any solution rationally attempted. Every logical solution remains unsatisfying, at the very least . . . Any movement out, any next step, is canceled, and the most dangerous temptation is to give up, to quit, to surrender to cynicism and despair, in the face of the disappointment, disenchantment, hopelessness, and loss of meaning that encompass one.[10]

Gays at an impasse will have difficulty with their self-worth and their self-image. They feel that they are a failure because of their orientation or because they have not been able to deal effectively with being gay. They may live in constant fear, depending on their role in society or their type of employment. In their case the feeling of rejection and lack of assurance which is part of the impasse is not merely something imagined. It is often their daily experience.

What is needed is what FitzGerald calls 'an imaginative shock'. That is, we find that our usual rational ways of thinking do not fit our sense of reality and so we need to move to a different level in order to maintain our lives. This is the more intuitive level of living. We must respond with full consciousness to our suffering with the belief that there is an opening to new possibilities ahead.[11] She notes:

> A genuine impasse situation is such that the more action one applies to escape it, the worse it gets. The principles of 'first order change' – reason, logic, analysis, planning – do not work . . . Thorough-going impasse forces one, therefore, to end one's habitual methods of acting by a radical breaking out of the conceptual blocks that normally limit one's thinking.[12]

Such impasse can be a place of growth and for the gays who are willing to enter into the experience, accept their limitations in the situation and are ready to give up control, whatever their dark night may be, it will be a time of growth and new life, of deepening their relationship with God, a hopeful experience of new possibilities ahead.

Very often this impasse comes about when gays fall in love. As this love moves to deeper and deeper levels, they experience the limits of love and they move through it to a new level of commitment and vision. Here we are not only talking about romantic love but all kinds of human love, including love of God. At some point we will come to an impasse

> with its intrinsic demands for and promise of a new vision, a new experience of God, a quieter, deeper, freer, more committed love. And it will come precisely when imagination seems paralyzed, when intimacy seems eroded, and when desire feels dead.[13]

The paradox is that the call to deeper intimacy comes when intimacy itself seems impossible to obtain. And so we are likely to think that this darkness is of our own making. Confronted with our own brokenness in all sorts of forms, it is not surprising that we experience a lack of self-esteem. But it is precisely in this experience of having no other place, no other thing to do, that faith can come into play. In fact what is going on despite the appearance is a transformation of the human person in love. And not only the transformation of the person, but ultimately of society and Christian theology.

There will be times when the impasse cannot be broken and the directee remains stuck. This could lead to a situation approaching despair. I think this would be rare. That there are no evident signs of movement out of impasse does not mean that nothing is happening. Some people are called to a kind of faith where there is little evidence of transformation. The new vision, the experience of God, which comes as a result of the impasse does not necessarily imply something which can be felt emotionally. I believe that this situation of living at an impasse may be what some chosen ones have as their way of being with God. It will feel like despair and working with these people will present directors with the greatest challenges to their sensitivity and discernment.

Out of such experiences theologians of gay theology will need to theologize. Such creative re-visioning must, like feminist spirituality, be based on the newly recognized experience of gay people. Gay men and women, by entering and going through their experiences of impasse, will be able to renew their images of God and rearticulate their religious experiences. FitzGerald's following words about the contemplative experience of women is equally true for gays:

> How imperative it is that women [gays] take possession of their pain and confusion; actively appropriate the experience of domination, exploitation, and oppression; consent to their time in history; and hold this impasse in their bodies and their hearts before the inner God they reach for in the dark of shattered symbols. Although the God of the dark night seems silent, this God is not a mute God who silences human desire, pain, and feeling, and women [gays] need to realize that the experience of anger, rage, depression, and abandonment is a constitutive part of the transformation and purification of the dark night.[14]

So then, beyond the universal call of God to bring us into relation with Godself, there is for gay persons a special reason to pursue the spiritual path. It has to do with their marginal status and the place of suffering in their lives precisely as these are experiences of limit. Obviously, there are others who are marginalized and suffering and, in some cases, even more so. They too need to develop that special relationship with the divine which we call the spiritual life.

It may seem that to frame the discussion of the need for a spiritual life in terms of suffering and marginalization is to prejudice it along negative lines. Should not this need be viewed along the more positive path of the goodness of gay persons as humans beings, such as how their bodies are incarnate manifestations of the Spirit working in the world, and how they have a place in the prophetic tradition of the Church?[15] But in spiritual direction we begin with the directee's actual existential situation. My experience is that gays (at all stages) in spiritual direction find that marginalization and suffering are relevant to their self-development as human beings pursued in a context of faith. And for many of them these negative experiences are the reasons they come to direction in the first place because they are real experiences of the dark night.[16] I develop the place of marginalization in the spiritual life below. The topic of suffering is discussed in the next chapter.

The marginalization of the gay person

From a social perspective marginal persons are those who have no social power. In various ways they have been excluded from society's ordinary way of proceeding. They have little or no voice in the dominant culture. They cannot effectively participate in responsible roles and do not have the power base to resolve their own issues in the public forum. They are those whose social and cultural positions are denigrated by the dominant majority culture. They are not integrated into society as a whole. Often marginality means being economically poor and living in under-developed circumstances. Through a process of conscientization marginal people can discover the source of their marginality and organize in order to overcome their powerlessness. Then, as Patrick Carroll, puts it:

> Marginal persons become agents of change. Integration, not incorporation, is the goal. Radical social change occurs when the creative subjectivity of marginal persons is empowered, acknow-ledged, and integrated into the dynamic social fabric.[17]

In terms of such a description the marginality of gays today requires some qualification. That they are marginalized is a fact which needs no documentation here. Consult your local newspaper, TV news reports, the struggles in the military and pending legislation in the states.[18] I know of no one who would maintain that gays are fully integrated in the Christian churches as the previous chapter distressingly makes clear. Some gays may also be marginalized by the fact that they are economically poor.

The other fact is that there is a growing awareness about the rights of gays. They are increasingly more politically organized, more sophis-ticated in making others aware of discrimination against them, and more courageous in being visible members of society. They are reclaiming their voices. Nevertheless, marginalization still exists and this will be a part, perhaps a major part, of spiritual direction with the gay person. The director will soon note how this experience can both inhibit spiritual growth and how this same spiritual process can make the journey through marginalization possible.

Michael Downey notes that the marginalized are those who live at the edges of or between the cracks of society. They are not part of the mainstream. People are marginalized in different ways due to their economic status, mental and physical handicaps, exclusion from church practices such as the divorced and remarried Catholics, and the oppression of women operating in a patriarchal society. Homosexuals are marginalized primarily because of gender or sexual identity. A good example of this is described in this quote from Marcus O'Donnell, who writes about the marginalized position of Australian gay men:

> Gay men present an interesting anomaly in the construction of sexuality and gender in society. We are *visible* as men and thus linked to dominant systems of patriarchal power but only in so far as our sexuality is kept *invisible*. Once seen as gay we quickly become identified with the marginalised, the other. This complex dynamic of both incorporation by and alienation from society frames the development of a gay man's world view.[19]

Downey notes that there are two major approaches to dealing with marginalization from the point of view of Christian spirituality. The first is that such marginality is temporary and is a stage of moving into the mainstream, a step in the process of taking on the norms and ways of understanding of the dominant group.[20] In my opinion this should not be the goal of any of the gay movements nor would it be healthy to take such a view in spiritual direction. But Downey sees a second approach:

> A second approach to the experience of marginalization recognizes marginalization as a permanent factor in the existence of some persons and groups. Together with this there is a recognition of the epistemological priority of the experience of those at the margins. This rests in the conviction that the life and ministry of Jesus were focussed on those at the margins of religious and social institutions to such a degree that he himself identified with them unto death and unto hell. In this view, Christ's Spirit is to be discerned in the struggle for liberation among those who have been cast to the margins of Church and society, making it possible to embrace marginalized existence itself as a primary locus of the Spirit's presence and action.[21]

This second approach contains in seminal form one of the main emphases of a spirituality for the gay person as well as it articulates one of the foundational points upon which a theology from a gay perspective is possible.

In dealing with gay directees directors would be remiss if they left the impression that their marginal state will disappear in their lifetime. Hopefully, the effects of it will be lessened. The process of spiritual direction should help gay individuals not only to be able to deal creatively with the status they find themselves in due to the various forms of homophobia, but also to affirm themselves as different in some way and to affirm that this difference has its own special contribution to make to the lives of others and to the larger culture. This permanent state of difference gives them a special vantage point from which to react to the larger culture and bestows on them certain qualities of sensitivity and insight which might be overlooked by the larger population unless something critical calls it to their attention.[22]

While it is true and of predominant importance that what we have in common as human beings is more significant than those areas where we differ, it is also true that people on the margins bring a perspective to the gospel proclamation and Christian living which is distinct. We are now more comfortable saying that there is a divine preference for the poor and dispossessed, that Christ focused his ministry on those pushed to the edges of society, that the Spirit of God is with the struggling oppressed peoples of the earth. Therefore, these people become a major source of theological reflection in our time.

Why cannot all these claims for the marginalized be made for those who are gay and lesbians in our world? Do they not also fulfil the qualifications for such a status because of their vulnerability? I believe they do. But what happens to all that if in spiritual direction the intent is to assist gay persons to understand themselves as just like the rest of all society, *except for a somewhat incidental difference regarding genital activity?* Justice here is not equivalent to bringing these people into the mainstream with the possibility of being co-opted by this same mainstream, causing them to lose the difference which bestows on them their prophetic voice.[23] For, if in fact our sexuality pervades our total selves, then there must be a difference which is characteristic of the total person when the sexual experience differs. It is precisely because gays/lesbians have this different experience, that it is possible to proceed to theologizing from a gay perspective.[24]

Despite the advances made, society's attitude toward homosexuality still places the gay person in a vulnerable position, especially the gay person who is trying to live a life characterized by openness to others according to gospel-orientated values. To be vulnerable often means that we find ourselves in a place where we are forced to retreat before certain forces in our lives. We are affected by certain things which happen to us or by certain people in our lives, and we have no way of preventing this. Spiritual direction is, first of all, meant to supply the support for the gay person who is having this experience. Part of direction is to find ways to counteract the deleterious effects of such an environment. But the idea is not to get rid of being a vulnerable person. Not only is that unrealistic, it is also contrary to the basic premise of Christianity whose founder's vulnerability requires no explication.

We are all vulnerable to some degree. It is part of being a human being. There are forces in all of our lives which can overwhelm us. Michael Downey notes that

> Our bodies, our selves, are really quite defenseless in the face of disease, sickness, suffering, accident and finally death, which claims the life of each human being . . . No matter how strong a person or group may be, there are the never-ending reminders that human life is very fragile, a gift, and the forces that bear upon it cannot be predicted or controlled.[25]

This means that vulnerability is a positive part of the spiritual life. Since Christ experienced vulnerability in his own life it does not seem possible to develop a spiritual life devoid of such an experience.

In the past I have written about the vulnerability of those marginalized by sickness and old age. I stressed that these people have a special vocation to the healthy and the powerful to remind them that not only are those qualities of health and power passing but also that there are deeper truths about being a full human being. Often those most vulnerable are those who are most sensitive to the more profound aspects of the person. In speaking about the power of the sacrament of anointing in the lives of the sick I noted that

> By giving substance to Christian hope for those in the Church who are well, the anointed person is participating in the establishment of the kingdom of God. The mission of the sick and the suffering Christian is to lift up what God is doing in her/his life to the rest of the Church so that all can see the power of God working in what appears to faithless eyes as absurdity at worst or as an unanswered question at best.[26]

By analogy,[27] I believe that other marginalized persons besides the sick and the elderly have a vocation in the Christian community to proclaim an aspect of the Christian faith which is hidden by our society's stress on such supposed values as being young, having a beautiful body, living without pain, or possessing power and influence. Such power may be obtained through money, but perhaps, more destructive is the power wielded by people because of position or education. Those who are vulnerable call this into question and say that in weakness lie true spiritual sources for meaning and happiness.

The gay person can be one of those who challenge those ruling presuppositions.[28] I see this as a great opportunity for gays committed to the spiritual life. They will need to become counter-cultural in two ways, to the culture of the larger Western middle-class society as well as to the gay subculture itself. Too often the dominant society's equivalence of the body beautiful with happiness and meaning are found in the gay subculture with a vengeance. Not everyone who works out at the gym is doing it to become a better human being. It is surprising how many gay directees still, at least subliminally, believe that happiness can be found if they can find someone who looks like the male model featured on the gay calendar. A large part of the movement for a deeper spiritual life for gay persons will need to deal with the issues of vulnerability not only because they are marginalized by the larger society but because they are called to challenge the values in the gay communities themselves.

It is understandable that those gays on the spiritual quest who find themselves in a vulnerable position that has been imposed on them by homophobic companions at work, by threatened friends or disappointed parents may want to pursue their growth in the Spirit along seemingly more positive lines.[29] They would hope that celebration would be the keynote of the spiritually committed gay person who has already suffered enough. They might resent any comparison to the sick and the elderly as a way of defining their prophetic call in life.[30] But that would be to try to escape the task of looking more deeply into who they are. Especially if they have already experienced being stripped naked of their dignity and find themselves alone, they might feel that to move more deeply still into these vulnerable areas will only result in seeing nothing but fear. Morton Kelsey puts it this way:

> This terror of looking directly into the void and finding only
> experiences that seem meaningless and devouring is worse than any

sickness. Yet the darkness is there. The need is not to escape it but to go through it and find meaning on the other side. There is still no better description of the darkness than the words of St. John of the Cross in *Dark Night of the Soul*.

The idea sometimes heard today that darkness can be avoided and we should find God only in joy and celebration, in peace and comfort, is a grave delusion that perhaps reveals our present lack of experience. We are apt either to begin this way in some darkness and depression or else be caught up by it somewhere along the way. Celebration is fine and comes after deliverance. Beforehand, celebration is often hollow, false, and naive.[31]

It would not be unusual for the director to find that gay people begin spiritual direction depressed and anxious. It may be that they are already looking at the inner darkness and are terrified and so seek help. At the same time that the director is supportive in this situation, it is equally important that s/he open up for gays and lesbians the possibility of reconnecting with their religious roots and finding that there is a transcendent dimension to their lives which can give meaning to such pain. But this presupposes the intentional pursuit of the spiritual journey. A humanizing response to marginality is not possible when the spiritual life is little more than an episodic experience.

To be marginalized does not mean that gays must be disconnected. Lack of connection and alienation may be what they experience as they begin their spiritual voyage. That will change and, as they continue to move to health, an increasing number of developmental connections will appear. When I suggest that the director help them reconnect with their religious roots I am not implying that the director encourage them to go to church. So many gay men and women have suffered because of the homophobia of their church that there is little possibility of a reconnection here. In fact, it might be destructive for them to try to do so. Many directors like myself who work in a church setting will have as a majority of directees gays who already work in the church scene in some way or who do not wish to sever their relationship with the institution. I suspect that they represent the majority of gays who are seeking what I call formal spiritual direction. But we also have directees who are not interested in connecting with the institutional church but come to us out of a deep spiritual hunger. Directors need to remember that religious roots are deeper and prior to any church. It is to that dimension of their lives that the director points these gay directees. It is not possible to predict how their continuing story will be fleshed out. We can, however, be their companions along whatever path opens up before them. It may be that out of these gays and lesbians groups may form. These groups may be 'church' for them, that is, their way of continuing their journey to God, but doing it together.

Notes

1   For a summary of some of the images of the spiritual life, including that of John of the Cross, see 'Journey (growth and development in spiritual life)', Michael Downey (ed.), *The New Dictionary of Catholic Spirituality* (Collegeville, MN: The Liturgical Press, A Michael Glazier Book, 1993), pp. 565–77. Other relevant articles in the same volume are: 'Darkness, dark night', 'Abandonment' and 'Negative way'. Those acquainted with the Ignatian tradition will easily make the connection with the experience of 'desolation'.

2   This theme is described by Herwig Arts SJ, in his book, *With your Whole Soul: On the Christian Experience of God* (New York: Paulist Press, 1983), pp. 88ff.

3   *Ibid.*, p. 90.

4   *Ibid.*, p. 91.

5   Gregory Baum, *Man Becoming* (New York: Herder and Herder, 1970). This has been a ground-breaking book. Although many of Baum's insights would be taken for granted now, nevertheless, his approach has been a singular influence on my own theology for the last quarter of a century. It bears rereading.

6   David Tracy, *Blessed Rage for Order* (New York: A Crossroad Book, 1975), p. 96. See this section of Tracy's work for what he calls the religious dimension of the limit experiences in our lives.

7   *Ibid.*, p. 105.

8   *Ibid.*, p. 105.

9   *Ibid.*, p. 105–6.

10   Constance FitzGerald, 'Impasse and dark night of the soul', in Joann Wolski Conn (ed.), *Women's Spirituality: Resources for Christian Development* (New York: Paulist Press, 1986), pp. 287–311 (p. 288). Sandra M. Schneiders has applied the notion of dark night to the experience of Roman Catholic women religious today which is similar to the work of FitzGerald. Schneiders puts the experience of the dark night in terms of women religious leaving behind a modernity of which they were not a part and entering a postmodernity for which they have not been prepared. See her 'Contemporary religious life: death or transformation?', *Cross Currents* (Winter 1996/7), pp. 510–35.

11   FitzGerald, 'Impasse', p. 290. This is very similar to the kind of language we use in conjunction with Sufi thinking, that is, we should not avoid our weakness, the dark parts of our lives, but rather go through them. We come out on the other side healthier people able to deal with the impasse as productive of something new.

12   *Ibid.*, p. 290. Ways of breaking out have been developed by Helen Palmer in her

work on attentional styles in her enneagram work. See especially *The Enneagram* (San Francisco: Harper and Row Publishers, 1988) and *The Enneagram in Love and Work* (HarperSanFrancisco, 1995). I would like to add my own work, *The Enneagram and Spiritual Direction: Nine Paths to Spiritual Growth* (New York: Continuum, 1997).

13 FitzGerald, 'Impasse', p. 292.

14 *Ibid.*, p. 306.

15 These are all issues which will find their place in the chapters ahead.

16 As desirable as it might be to avoid what for some appears as a less than uplifting (i.e. negative) consideration of the need of a spiritual life for gay persons, it is important that I write out of my own experience in doing direction with gays. Thus far, I have not had anyone come into my office and begin the session with 'I feel wonderful about being gay. Let's talk about all the ways I can continue to rejoice in that fact.' Sometimes the person can say that after an often long and almost always struggling process of self-appropriation.

17 Patrick Carroll, 'Marginal persons', Judith A. Dwyer (ed.), *The New Dictionary of Catholic Social Thought* (Collegeville: The Liturgical Press, 1994), p. 563.

18 For a description of how gays are kept in the 'closet' at various levels of life in America see Michelangelo Signorile, *Queer in America: Sex, The Media, and the Closets of Power* (New York: Random House, 1993). Many would not be comfortable with his statement 'I consider truthful discussion of the lives of homosexual public figures as legitimate and significant in the larger aim to give courage to millions of gay people who stay in the closet out of fear and shame' (ix). Rik Isensee says: 'Growing up gay in a homophobic culture is comparable to growing up in a dysfunctional family.' See his *Growing up Gay in a Dysfunctional Family* (New York: Prentice Hall Press, 1991).

19 Quoted in *Don't Leave Me this Way: Art in the Age of Aids*, compiled by Ted Gott (Melbourne: National Gallery of Australia, 1994), p. 29.

20 Downey, 'The marginalized', in *The New Dictionary of Catholic Spirituality*, pp. 623–4.

21 *Ibid.*, p. 624.

22 I am fully aware that many gays and lesbians and straight people who are open to them would not agree with me on this point. Some optimistically assume that there will come a time when gays will be 'just like everyone else', and their sexuality will be irrelevant to the larger society. Perhaps, they are right. However, I also find that those who espouse this more optimistic view are reluctant to give up the special perspective gays may have on human life and the human response to God. I do not believe that we can have it both ways. For more on this topic see Urvashi Vaid, *Virtual Equality: The Mainstreaming of Gay and Lesbian Liberation* (New York: Anchor Books, 1995). For a discussion which avoids the extremes of total absorption of gayness into the mainstream and the over identification with a group see Leo Bersani, *Homos* (Cambridge, Mass.: Harvard University Press, 1995).

23 This despite the fact that a lot of homosexuals would like to be floating along in that same mainstream to enjoy all of its advantages. Some even hope that homosexuality will become mainstream.

24 The possibility of a feministic theology is based upon a similar presupposition about

the difference of women's experience. This difference is not so absolute that it diminishes the common humanity that men and women share, but it is significant enough that if it is not taken into account in theology and the spiritual life, serious misjudgements can be made.

25 Downey, 'Weakness and vulnerability', *The New Dictionary of Catholic Spirituality*, p. 1019.

26 James Empereur SJ, *Prophetic Anointing: God's Call to the Sick, the Elderly, and the Dying* (Collegeville, The Liturgical Press, Michael Glazier Series, 1982), pp. 158–9.

27 This analogy is made for the purpose of establishing the vocational quality of marginal people. It does not imply that the cause of this vulnerability is a kind of sickness.

28 This usually means that the gay person is publicly known as gay or lesbian.

29 Homophobia is the main reason for the marginalization of the gay person as it is also a main reason for the cause of suffering in their lives. I will take that up more explicitly in the section on suffering.

30 I would presume that those with AIDS or directly working with those with AIDS would find the comparison even more poignant.

31 Morton Kelsey, *Transcend: A Guide to the Spiritual Quest* (New York: Crossroad, 1981), p. 92.

4

The gay person's passage through suffering

The absence of God and suffering[1]

Given the context in which direction with the gay person takes place today, it would be unusual to have a directee who is not experiencing suffering in his or her life.[2] How the person is dealing with it will depend upon the stage of their adult development, a topic which I will consider later. In a book to which I have already referred, *With Your Whole Soul: On the Christian Experience of God*, Herwig Arts SJ describes the place of suffering in religious experience. He says it is not to be 'attributed to masochism, nor to a morbid mysticism of the cross'.[3] Rather, suffering is found where there is great love or the great longing for the beloved. It is the inaccessibility and absence of the lover which causes the love to grow in passion. He says that a unity which cannot be achieved actually stimulates longing, a kind of suffering. Arts applies this to the person's experience of God who is incomprehensible and so inaccessible. But God is not completely so. The reason the human heart is so restless for God is that it has tasted some of this love. The more we taste this love, the hungrier the human spirit is. 'Not missing God at all, being able to get along very well without God, is only the lot of those who haven't the least glimmer of a notion who God is.'[4]

Absence is not the same as sterility or non-existence. Arts notes that to experience the desert does not mean that I am experiencing nothing. It means that God is not experienced continually at every moment of life. Today, it may be more helpful to speak of the absence of God when our awareness of the presence of God is so ambiguous. This absence need not be considered a sign of spiritual emptiness. It often is the breaking down of restrictive images of God from our past. This passage through absence, then, is a necessary liberation in spiritual growth. Deprivation of the presence of God is the most effective destroyer of our pre-suppositions, our idols of who God is and what we are experiencing when we experience God. There is deep pain in this passage. How can it be otherwise? It is this very pain which makes it possible for us to experience real love. Arts asks: 'Can we ever explain what love is if the person to whom we speak claims to have been feeling just fine for years, living totally wrapped up in his or her own self?'[5]

It may be that spiritual direction will begin with someone who is experiencing this absence of God and who will need the clarifying support to find meaning where now such meaning is gone. What once created a feeling of connection with God no longer does. It is as if they have lost God. The usual points of contact with God no longer fulfil that function. The director's task will be to show the significance of these present experiences and to help the directee to see the wisdom in what Arts says on this point:

> A relationship traveling only on the stream of remarkable experiences never reaches the stable shores of faithful love. Without the dreadful night of suffering from absence, faithful friendship remains an unknown land. We have to miss a certain friend badly a few times before we can discover who this friend really is.[6]

My own experience does indicate that there are gay persons who come to direction with such an experience of suffering because of this seeming spiritual emptiness and who wish to address it. But, on the surface at least, the suffering that the majority of gays experience is in terms of the absence of a relationship, often the absence of a present or former lover. Their belief in God may be quite strong, often articulated in a traditional, even overly personalistic way. Their problems with God have more to do with the attitudes of Christians toward gays, although for some this would be but a surface experience covering a deeper disquiet about God. Their suffering is articulated more along the lines of temporary or permanent separation from a lover, whether in its beginning or final stages. This same suffering may reveal an absence of God in their lives. Helping the directee deal with the absence of a lover and its attendant suffering will be, in fact, to help them deal with the absence of God in their lives.

I do not want to suggest that the pain of an ended or interrupted relationship is an issue with every gay person coming to direction. Nor do I think this is usually the main issue. Frequently, the absence has to do not so much with a lover but with parents, friends at work, the lack of community support, or feeling the need for some significant intimacy.[7] Nor is some kind of absence the only source of suffering in the gay person's life. There may be greater causes of suffering,[8] but suffering there is and it is important that gay persons have clear spiritual resources to draw upon to integrate the suffering parts of their lives.

Often dealing with the absence of God is to deal, then, with the absence of a lover. The question of the lover gives the director the opportunity to explore with the directees their relationship with God. Arts points out that when we are dealing with establishing contact with a person, whether divine or human the same questions arise:

> What am I really looking for, the person of my beloved with *his* or *her* feelings, longings, and uniqueness, or *my* experience of the beloved? Am I looking for my spouse or am I looking for an erotic sensation? Am I looking for God, or am I seeking purely my devotion, key spiritual rest, or my psychological well-being? Am I seeking the other, or am I seeking my experience? If the latter is true, I may indeed speak of love, but what I am looking for is myself.[9]

We destroy love by concentrating on ourselves rather than the other. This is such a truism. But the fact is that before the director can reflect in any depth with the directee regarding the latter's love of God, it will be necessary to look at whether there is in the present experience of the directee the experience of being in love with love. When we are in love with love, it is our own desires and longings which are the focus of our attention. We then demand that the loved ones be present, not as they are in themselves, but as objects of love in the same way as our desires and longings are. In other words, there is no place for absence in this relationship. And once the feelings drop away, the relationship fades away. When being in love with love is confused with real human love, then a felt experience of God is confounded with an authentic relationship with God.

Relishing devotion has no more to do with belief than sexual awakening for an adolescent has to do with married love. To seek experience for the sake of experience is to seek oneself. To seek the other on account of that other is to experience love.[10]

Clarifying this issue in direction will help the director to sense whether the directee is seeking God or seeking an experience of God. These need not be mutually exclusive and we might ask how one can go without the other. But they can and they must at times. Just as the absence of the lover can bring directees to distinguish between being in love with love and being in love with another, so this same absence of a lover can help them to know if they love God or the presence of God. Of course, this depends on whether they can make the transfer from the absence of the lover to the absence of God. Why is this important? Because for persons who find themselves marginalized, and certainly, when so for reasons of gender, and for whom suffering in life is present, it is important to find the salvational value in absence, whether this is absence of God or of a relationship. There would be greater clarity and far fewer complications in the spiritual life if people knew if they were in love with God or in love with their experience of God. Here my presupposition is that in order to find out whether we truly love God we need to know if we are truly loving another human being.

The experienced director or counsellor knows that in the actual experiences of directees it is not so easy to distinguish authentic love of another and of God from those feelings which are more self-referential. After all, even our feelings for others and for God are still our own. The great mystery of human love, even when directed to God, is that while it is the cause of union between lover and beloved, it is still a very individual thing. Here especially directors should try to free themselves from any presuppositions which would lead them to treat all directees alike. For some directees their real issue will be the absence of the lover. For others it may be the loss that is the result of a relationship which they may have ended for healthy reasons. Fear of intimacy may be the main obstacle for others, although usually such fear is present along with the other issues.

The purpose of my previous cautionary remarks on distinguishing being in love with love from genuine love is that they are precisely that, cautions for the director. It is not to over-simplify the process of growing into true love which develops often through many and complicated stages, one of which is being in love with love. It is not to deny that love is a 'many-splendoured' experience. Our loving is as the English Jesuit poet, Gerard Manley Hopkins, put it, a 'Pied Beauty', a 'dappled thing'. It is 'counter, original, spare, strange'. It is 'fickle . . . swift, slow; sweet, sour; adazzle, dim'.[11] In our growing into that kind of love of which the gospel speaks – love of God through love of neighbour by loving ourselves – we are all like Hopkins as he watched the falcon in the morning air pushing against the wind while gliding along with it. As the poet was caught up in the mastery, the achievement of the Windhover riding on the air, an act of 'brute beauty and valour and act', he wrote: 'My heart in hiding stirred for a bird.'[12] The process of growing in love for all of us, gay and straight, is to bring our hearts out of hiding. Most of us have to do it by making the passage through romantic love. It is the noble task of spiritual direction to help directees to bring their hearts 'out of hiding'.

Gays, loving God or loving their experience of God?

Many would respond that this question is equally true for both homosexuals and heterosexuals. And, of course, that is true. All people who want to have a relationship with God must be able to distinguish their love of God from their feelings about loving God and from the experience of *wanting to love God*. But there are some differences for homosexuals. For instance, for the gay man the absence of the lover (in the stricter sense) which provides a way of finding the meaning in the absence of God happens to be another man. This absence calls up all the other attendant absences that he may have in his life. To put it simplistically, when a straight man is missing the woman in his life, he can usually rely on the people in his life to sympathize and support him. It is far more questionable that a gay man will have an identical experience. And that is a relatively superficial concern (although not emotionally) when compared with the difference when a gay man relates to God through another man rather than through a woman. The difference will resonate through the particular man in question, in the other man, and in the ways they both image God.[13]

Most Christians, certainly those explicitly interested in a spiritual life, are familiar with the Augustinian dictum that our hearts are restless until they rest in God. Like most spiritual aphorisms it has been more misinterpreted than not. For some this has meant that they can bypass human love and the human lover and move directly to God. I suppose that there are those who have such a special calling from God, but to make that into a general principle would seem to trivialize the Incarnation. If God thought it such a great idea to connect with us through a human, bodily and sexual person such as Jesus of Nazareth, why should we presume that moving to God through relationships which are human, bodily and sexual is not an equally good idea? But if this is such a good idea, then, it is even more important to be able to distinguish in our search for love (a lover?) which we all have, between the experience of love itself and the God that we love. To put it simply, in my desire to love God am I concerned about God and about God's happiness? Can I love God only in the felt experience of God which personally satisfies me or do I also love God in the absence and suffering? My experience of the beloved should give me the clue to my love of God.

There are clues to know whether we are in love with God or not. They are of two kinds. The first is when we love God as God loves us and the second is when we love God as we love others. Clues of the first kind are found wherever God has been working. For instance, in the Old Testament we see how God loves through the gifts God bestowed on Israel. God's love in the New Testament is manifested through Jesus himself who is the greatest gift, through the kingdom of God beginning among us, and through the suffering involved in taking up the cross of Christ. As regards the second kind of clues found in the way we love others, no better description can found than that in the Scriptures. In particular I refer to Paul's first letter to the Corinthians 13:4–7:

> Love is patient; love is kind. Love is not jealous, it does not put on airs, and it is not snobbish; it is never rude or self seeking; it is not prone to anger, nor does it brood over injuries. Love doesn't rejoice in what is wrong, but rejoices in the truth. There is no limit to love's forbearance, to its trust, its hope, its power to endure.[14]

The suffering caused by prejudice

The suffering coming from love, while real and significant in the life of gay people, may not be obvious. What is clear to both gays and straights is the amount of suffering which is the result of prejudice and the misconceptions people have about gays and lesbians. We can remove this faulty understanding by providing information. That is the basic conclusion of Jeannine Gramick in her study of 'Prejudice and religion and homosexual people'.[15] In her article she employs sociological findings to show that religious people who are often rigidly biased against homosexuals are that way not so much because of religion but because of a deeper cultural homophobia. Her point is that although religion has been and is seen as the enemy of lesbians and gays and their lifestyles, religion itself is not the cause of their oppression. I suspect she agrees with Boswell who claims that societal homophobia makes use of religion to justify its prejudice and animosity towards homosexuals.[16] In other words, the condemnatory attitude of right-wing Christians regarding homosexuality and homosexual behaviour comes more from the fact that these Christians are operating out of their being deeply infected by society's uncomfortableness with gays and lesbians. They use theological language and rely on biblical passages to justify their prejudice, but in fact they are not responding to the central teachings of Jesus. The Church is the instrument of such homophobia, not the cause of it. Gramick says:

> If Christianity is the conduit rather than the cause of homosexual prejudice, and if religious beliefs are used merely to disguise or to give a semblance of rationality to already deeply rooted feelings of intolerance, then future researchers must ask, 'What *are* the factors responsible for anti-gay prejudice?'[17]

This is not to say that the churches are not homophobic or that they should be excused of the presence of homophobic elements in their midst. Rather, she points to several areas where further research is required and sees the alleviation of many of these culturally embedded elements of homophobia and of homosexual oppression through education. The world sets the agenda for the Church and influences the Church's response to cultural issues more often than many of us Christians would like to admit.

But how can we defend ourselves against prejudice? Is education enough? 'What distinguishes prejudice from a simple misconception is *emotional resistance to new evidence.*'[18] A person operating from a prejudiced viewpoint categorizes others and assigns negative qualities to them. Facts are irrelevant or are given a twisted interpretation to support the bias. There is a great deal of quiet suffering among gays because, although they may not be public about their orientation, they are automatically placed in a group of people who are out to destroy the family, are paedophiles, carriers of a deadly disease, and have no boundaries in the area of sexual practice. This is especially painful for practising Christians (and other religious people) when such bias is manifested by other Christians. In many ways this cause of suffering is more intense now despite the advances in consciousness-raising in this area. Previously, prejudicial jokes about gays were told in a more limited atmosphere since they ranked close to 'dirty jokes'. Now with the discussion of gays in the military, the movement against same-sex unions, and the question of the ordination of gays and lesbians in the churches, gays can easily encounter a less crudely expressed form of prejudice, one seemingly based on 'family values', the morale of soldiers, and the will of Christ for the Church. Being more sophisticated in expression does not lessen the cruel power of the categorization. It is still dismissive of the full humanity of the gay person and so still a source of pain. In fact, the suffering is intensified because the sources should know better. This is especially true when the pain is inflicted by family members, long-time friends, and the religious community. This is true for all gays, but may be intensified when they are public about their sexual orientation.

We cannot discount the effect of public discussions on the individual gay person. The gay directee may not be a member of the military but he or she does have to deal with certain public judgements made by that segment of society. Scanzoni and Mollenkott deal with the deleterious effects of such public caricatures when they refer to the case of Tracy Thorne, the highly qualified navy lieutenant, who was dismissed from the navy upon his admission of his homosexual orientation.

> He found especially disturbing the efforts of the religious right to 'distort the debate by linking homosexuality with everything from pedophilia to a maniacal lack of sexual self control'. Decrying the portrayal of gay and lesbian people as 'sexual predators' whose primary aim is to lure their heterosexual colleagues into sexual liaisons, he argued that the notion 'that homosexuals lack self-control is a myth based in fear and ignorance'.[19]

There are few good role models for the gay person. Some of them wear the military uniform. When people who have served their country in a public and outstanding way, which has been recognized by the military itself, are humiliated by the same institution bringing to an end their careers and hopes for the future, this can have a negative effect on those not part of that institution. Such negativity floating about in the public air is like smog poisoning the atmosphere in which the directee lives. It does not help when the government or military suppress the results of studies which indicate that sexual orientation is not relevant to job performance.[20] It has been suggested that the military treat homosexuals as a minority group so that sexual discrimination can be handled in a fashion similar to racial prejudice. Even if the US military had accepted this recommendation, which it has not, the sense of marginalization with its attendant pain would still be there. Only now the suffering would be the result of a minority status rather than gender related. It is an unhappy fact that even in religious communities, especially of men, some of the gay members are 'outed' by other members of the same community. Although these 'outed' members are not expelled from the group, a certain kind of marginalization does occur. For instance, they may become unacceptable to hold certain positions in the community and in the institutions sponsored by the community.

I see no way of avoiding the suffering that comes from being a person 'not like others'. Spiritual direction can help diminish the effects, assist the directee through the difficult passages involved, and open the interior resources which are needed to live in such an atmosphere. But the fact remains that homosexuality represents the opposite of what the military and Church stand for: 'order, authority, and convention'.[21] Being gay and lesbian can only threaten those whose identity is tied to certain ways of acting and living, to certain rules of conduct which must be adhered to, and who operate according to fixed stereotypes of what it means to be masculine or feminine. For men who want to be men and who think they know what it is to be a man, the presence of gay men is profoundly disturbing. Most gay men in spiritual direction have some notion that they are in that sense counter-cultural, that they have a disturbing effect on some men.[22] Knowing that this is often the case because these men do not have their own sexuality integrated in their lives or that they are defining their manhood in terms of control over women may help the directee to understand intellectually what is happening.[23] But it still hurts a gay man to know that he threatens other men when he does not intend to and in fact would like to have a harmonious relationship with these men. Because of the pervasiveness of this attitude, any experienced director will be able to recite a litany of seemingly trifling details from the daily life of the directees which have caused them pain. The authors Scanzoni and Mollenkott summarize the dilemma for the homosexual in the larger culture this way:

> There is something going on, too, in the anxieties many people express about homosexuality. Homosexuality is a phenomenon outside most people's frame of reference, and many are not ready to make room for it in their way of viewing the world. It is not something they understand, and what people don't understand they often fear. Many people find it unsettling to question beliefs they have taken for granted. They cling desperately to familiar ways of thinking. And they want to make sure their children grow up seeing the world as they do.[24]

Living with AIDS and the concept of suffering

I could never adequately catalogue all the sources of suffering for gays and lesbians or any other group of persons. One about which we cannot be silent is also one which has moved so many gays to pursue the spiritual life with more intensity. That is AIDS. This disease afflicts so many people and not only gays.[25] But it has caused such destruction among gays that most will know of someone who has AIDS or who has died of it. For directors who work with people who are HIV positive or who have AIDS, I would recommend that they familiarize themselves with Richard L. Smith's book, *AIDS, Gays, and the American Catholic Church.*[26] Smith begins his first chapter with these words:

> AIDS is so much more than a matter of microbes. It is also a matter of human suffering . . . More than simply a matter of bodily fluids, viral infections and treatment regimens, AIDS is also a complex web of conflicting emotions – rage and fear and grief, tenderness and courage. It is also a matter of human values – justice, compassion, loyalty, pride in one's identity, and love. AIDS is more than 'the story of a virus', as the National Academy of Sciences once termed it.[27]

It is not that there is a special perspective on AIDS that comes from the practice of Christian spiritual direction. But it will be a large part of the journey of many gays and this needs to be recognized. Two things can and should happen here. First, the director can affirm Smith's assessment about the larger world of AIDS. I suspect that most directors would want to deal with the several emotions mentioned by Smith. And second, these various emotions can become passages to a new level of commitment and a distinct way of experiencing God.[28] The beginning experience in direction may be profoundly disturbing in the case of the gay directee whose lover has recently died. Such loss is often destructive of faith itself as chronicled by Felice Picano, a baptized Catholic, who describes his experience of rejecting traditional Christianity because of its position on homosexuality, finding in Buddhism a kind of meaning for his life, but then hoping for some kind of afterlife when his lover of sixteen years died. He admits that he longs for the Christian afterlife for his lover which resembles more the Christian belief than that of Buddhism. His description of how he feels despite his present beliefs will be something many a director will encounter:

> In a strangely oblique way, I've achieved something akin to that balance the *I Ching* speaks of as required for the Superior Man, that objective compassion Buddhists seek for enlightenment. Yet oddly enough, I don't feel any peace. Most days I feel irritated and sad. If there is a deity, I now know that She/He/It is *not* my particular friend; too often has She/He/It been my enemy, thwarted my wishes and needs for some other end She/He/It required. In truth I've felt manipulated, pushed around. And I'll say it, I don't really care for my life any more. It's lost its value to me. I'd throw it away on a whim . . . [29]

AIDS as well as homosexuality in general will present a clear opportunity for the director to examine the role that metaphors play in the life of the directee. I have noted that Seubert has called for an extension of our metaphorical understanding to include the homosexual experience. Smith too deals with metaphors because, following the sociological position that reality is socially constructed, he explicates an American Catholic construction of AIDS.[30] He agrees with Susan Sontag who points up the destructive results when one treats illness as a metaphor, that we must take seriously the biological data regarding AIDS and that it must be treated as a disease and not some kind of punishment from God. Smith says of Sontag:

> She exposes the longstanding cultural stereotypes – racist, homo-phobic stereotypes, often with a bias against Third World peoples

– lurking within our metaphors of AIDS. She hopes to free people of the oppressive cultural overlays we put on AIDS, to present AIDS as 'just a disease'.[31]

Here Smith parts company with Sontag. For him, AIDS is not just a disease. The biomedical model of AIDS may remove some of the religiously judgemental views of AIDS which oppress the person who has it by branding him or her as a sinner. But the medical model carries its own form of oppression, such as the use of a painful medical technique which may be of no value to the patient. The biomedical model cannot deal with those questions which come up at this time: Why do I have this disease? Why is this happening to me and what does it mean? Smith makes a very good point when he says: 'Asking *why* one has a disease is not the same as asking *how* one contracted it.'[32] It is the *why* that will be an important part of direction.[33]

Search for new metaphors of the meaning of gay spirituality and suffering

So much of human suffering comes from our being dominated by certain metaphors. So much that we do in spiritual direction has to do with the metaphors that guide people's lives. Sometimes old metaphors must be discarded; sometimes new ones must be provided. Suffering may be a good place to begin the search for new metaphors that can be constructive of the world-view of the gay directee. Smith notes:

> Metaphors frame the similarities between one set of experiences and another. In doing this, they give shape and meaning to our experiences and precisely because they limit our field of vision, orienting us to see some rather than other aspects of our experience, and to do so in one way rather than another.
>
> So it is with metaphors for AIDS. They both reveal and hide certain aspects of our experience. They shape the way in which we approach the experience of AIDS. Some metaphors empower people to approach AIDS with a certain gracefulness and determination to live fully and actively; other metaphors (such as Jerry Falwell's 'Divine punishment' metaphor and Patrick Buchanan's secular counterpart to it: 'nature's retribution') can cripple people with inappropriate anxiety, guilt, and alienation. Not all metaphors of AIDS are of equal value.[34]

This is very significant for spiritual direction because it is precisely our metaphors which put us in contact with God. How can one pursue the spiritual life unless one enters into the greatest metaphor of all, Jesus Christ, where the divine and human come together, realities which do not naturally go together. This search for new metaphors will provide the directors with an opportunity to look at the operative metaphors in their own lives. The debilitating ones will have to be jettisoned. The directee will need assistance to name and claim the metaphors of his or her life. And the director will most probably be doing the same thing at the same time. Only then can the relationship be productive. Not only will this bring about the possibility that gay persons will integrate suffering in their lives, finding meaning there, but this will open up the larger process of developing those images, symbols and metaphors that will be the positive structure of the spiritual life of the gay directees.

As I have noted more than once, Xavier John Seubert has addressed this matter of the need to develop new metaphors to include the rich possibilities of the gay life most explicitly. However, these metaphors do not spring into existence from nowhere. They are born of the lives of those gays who affirm their own goodness. Seubert sees the new metaphor of homosexuality from a sacramental point of view. This presupposes that Christian gays can affirm themselves in church and that the Christian community listens to them. When gays experience their sexuality and eroticism as a way of being open to life, as a way of loving more fully, they are engaging in a sacramental process. For Seubert the usual distinction between orientation and act does not function from a sacramental point of view because

> The distinction between orientation and act presumes that once sexual desire is quarantined and contained, the homosexual person is just like anyone else. This terribly naive presumption does much damage to persons both in their lives and in their deaths. It damages their lives, because it denies them a part of the *sacramentum* – an important aspect of the ability to receive, embody and put presence into effect.[35]

The matter of discovering more adequate metaphors to understand homosexuality is a project that most spiritual directors of gays will be engaged in informally and implicitly. It happens every time we help gay directees to experience their goodness, every time we assist them in their struggle to articulate better the presence of God in their lives so that their experience of God will be more accessible to them and more available to the larger society. Seubert emphasizes a sobering and powerful truth when he says that the metaphors we live by are those by which we die. I do not think it an overstatement to say that what we directors do in spiritual direction comes under the larger category of the formulation of new metaphors for our gay directees. Gay men and women will live by some kind of metaphors whether they have been created, inherited, imposed or borrowed. They will either live creatively according to them or they will be diminished by them. Spiritual directors will be called upon to help all directees to reforge the metaphors by which they journey to God, but in the case of gay persons this task is rendered awesome because as Seubert says:

> Metaphors are a matter of life and death. And the best thing we can do for people in life and death is to give them metaphors by which they understand how they are loved, how they are able to love, and how every dimension of their beings can be creative of life.[36]

Notes

1   It is not my intent to give a survey of all the sources of suffering in the gay person pursuing the spiritual life. What I present are some areas by way of example, but areas which are significant in the direction process, usually in the earlier stages.

2   An important part of discernment will be to recognize to what degree this suffering is coming from outside sources such as societal homophobia and to what degree it is self-inflicted.

3   Herwig Arts SJ, *With Your Whole Soul: The Christian Experience of God* (New York: Paulist Press, 1983), p. 80.

4   *Ibid.*, p. 81.

5   *Ibid.*, p. 83.

6   *Ibid.*

7   For the various kinds of loss experienced by gay people and the need for care at these times see Larry Kent Graham, 'The desolation of our habitations', Chapter 5 of *Discovering Images of God* (Westminister/John Knox Press, 1997).

8   One of the great sources of pain for gays and lesbians comes from feeling excluded and so silenced. Marilyn Bennett Alexander and James Preston graphically portray what this feels like in their book, *We Were Baptized Too: Claiming God's Grace for Lesbians and Gays* (Louisville, KY: Westminster/John Knox Press, 1996). They indicate how exclusion causes a distorted image of God and self, a distorted view of the body of Christ and our place in it, and a dysfunctional search for intimacy with

its attendant rage. Some directees may profit from the stories the authors relate of individuals who have felt the pain of silence and exclusion. Sometimes the usual talk of spiritual direction is best substituted by art and literature. For more stories of suffering in the concrete lives of gays and lesbians see Leanne McCall Tigert, *Coming Out While Staying In* (Cleveland: United Church Press, 1996). See Chapter 6, 'Stories of hurting, stories of healing: lesbian, gay, and bisexual persons speak of their experiences in the Church'. Through these interviews with members of the United Church of Christ the author wishes to demonstrate the 'significant relationship between psychological and theological/spiritual liberation'.

9   *Ibid.*, p. 84.

10 *Ibid.*, p. 85.

11 These are some of the images Hopkins uses in his poem, 'Pied Beauty', W. H. Gardner (ed.), *Gerard Manley Hopkins: A Selection of His Poems and Prose* (Baltimore: Penguin Books, 1962), pp. 30–1.

12 *Ibid.*, p. 30. Hopkins considered 'The Windhover' his greatest poem.

13 This is a subtle and complicated matter. It is part of the basic experience upon which gay theology depends. Its treatment must be left for another time. I do not wish to be misunderstood here. Of course, gay men can and do relate to God through the significant women in their lives. I trust the reader understands the point I am trying to make here.

14 Translation taken from *The Inclusive New Testament* (Brentwood, MD: Priests for Equality, 1994). Some other references are 2 Corinthians 5:19ff. and the Good Samaritan (Luke 10). These ideas about love are further developed by Elizabeth Dreyer in 'Love', Michael Downey (ed.), *The New Dictionary of Catholic Spirituality* (Collegeville, MN: The Liturgical Press, 1993), pp. 612–622.

15 In Robert Nugent (ed.), *A Challenge to Love: Gay and Lesbian Catholics in the Church* (New York: Crossroad, 1986).

16 *Ibid.*, p. 11.

17 *Ibid.*, p. 13.

18 From Letha Dawson Scanzoni and Virginia Ramey Mollenkott, *Is the Homosexual My Neighbor?* (HarperSanFrancisco, revised edn, 1994), p. 158. The authors are employing the work of the psychologist Gordon Allport here. For more on this see 'Gay suffering and the promise of immortality', Frank B. Leib, *Friendly Competitors, Fierce Companions: Men's Ways of Relating* (Cleveland: The Pilgrim Press, 1997), pp. 174–94.

19 *Ibid.*, p. 160.

20 *Ibid.*, p. 167.

21 *Ibid.*, p. 171.

22 It does not help when some gay men exaggerate the percentage of gays in society or too readily assume that the other guy is gay.

23 For an eloquent expression of this issue see Bruce Bawer, *A Place at the Table* (New York: Simon & Schuster, 1994), pp. 116–20. A revealing phenomenon is the fact that some men are threatened by common showers with gay men. Bawer notes: 'One reporter after another discovered that servicemen who were trained to be cool under fire were unsettled by the thought of a homosexual glancing their way in a shower ... What bothered them was the idea of *knowing* ... All that could make such a

situation more uncomfortable for him is the idea that one of those other men might be sexually attracted to him – might want (as many a young straight man tends to think of it) to use him as woman' (p. 118).

24 *Ibid.*, p. 175. This lack of understanding of homosexuality has been discussed from a more theological perspective by Xavier John Seubert OFM in his article, 'The sacramentality of metaphors: reflections on homosexuality', *Cross Currents* (Spring 1991), pp. 52ff. Seubert argues for the extension of the metaphorical process, that our present metaphors are not comprehensive enough to 'include the rich possibilities of gay and lesbian life', and that there is need for metaphors which will allow a place for the homosexual experience in human life and the Church.

25 For the stories of the many different kinds of people who live with HIV/AIDS see Neal Hitchens, *Voices That Care: Stories and Encouragements for People with AIDS/HIV and Those Who Love Them* (Los Angeles: Lowell House, 1992). For a treatment of issues connected with AIDS but given little attention, such as ethical issues for women with AIDS, see Julien S. Murphy, *The Constructed Body: AIDS, Reproductive Technology, and Ethics* (New York: SUNY Press, 1996).

26 Richard L. Smith, *AIDS, Gays, and the American Catholic Church* (Cleveland: The Pilgrim Press, 1994), foreword by Robert Bellah. For those directees who are more aesthetically inclined and for whom the aesthetic experience is a source of meaning and comfort, I recommend books such as the one referred to earlier, Ted Gott (ed.), *Don't Leave Me this Way: Art in the Age of Aids* (Melbourne: National Gallery of Australia, 1994), which deals with the various aspects of the AIDS epidemic through visual art. For the testimony of one priest's struggle with people with HIV/AIDS and how we find God even in the midst of struggles see Robert Arpin, *Wonderfully, Fearfully Made* (San Francisco: Harper, 1993). A friend of mine, Jack Miffleton, was very instrumental in bringing this book to publication.

27 Smith, *AIDS, Gays, and the American Catholic Church*, p. 7.

28 See Michael Kearney MD, *Mortally Wounded: Stories of Soul Pain, Death, and Healing* (New York: Scribner, 1996). The author deals with suffering and AIDS and his thesis is that most of what we experience in terms of suffering is connected to a soul wound and taking the person to that soul wound and healing it allows suffering, marginalization and rejection to be redemptive and allows the person the gift of letting go and being at peace. He explains how it is possible to learn how to die well and accept death as an integral part of the journey of life. Several examples deal with those with HIV/AIDS.

29 Felice Picano, 'AIDS: The new crucible of faith', in Brian Bouldrey (ed.), *Wrestling with the Angel: Faith and Religion in the Lives of Gay Men* (New York: Riverhead Books, 1995), p. 281. Dawna Markova, *No Enemies Within: A Creative Process for Discovering What's Right About What's Wrong* (Berkeley: Conari Press, 1994) can be helpful in dealing with pain as a teacher rather than an enemy.

30 Smith's work here has implications for a much wider audience than Catholics. His concern is to show the paradoxical position towards AIDS that the Catholic Church has, that is, on the one hand, it places AIDS in the context of its moral teaching regarding homosexual acts and, on the other hand, it encourages a compassionate pastoral approach to those with AIDS. For Smith, the AIDS epidemic brings together the Catholic community and the gay culture in such a way that a common

conversation between the two might be possible. The two sides, although in conflict, have a common goal of alleviating human suffering in this epidemic. For a discussion of how the US Catholic hierarchy can maintain a clear position regarding the sinfulness of homosexual activity while allowing a certain freedom to those who work with gay men living with HIV/AIDS, see Mark Kowalewski, *All Things to All People: The Catholic Church Confronts the Aids Crisis* (Albany: SUNY Press, 1994).

31   Smith, *AIDS, Gays, and the American Catholic Church*, p. 9.

32   *Ibid.*, p. 15.

33   There are other good resources for the director who works with people who either are positive, have AIDS or are people who work with those who do. Some of these are: Paul Tucker, *Christian Caring: Four Models of HIV/AIDS Ministry in the Local Church* (Los Angeles: Universal Fellowship Press, 1994), a manual with various models of ministry to HIV/AIDS persons. Tucker divides his manual according to the three major losses: of dreams (asymptomatic HIV), of healthiness (symptomatic HIV), and of independence (debilitating HIV); see also: *HIV/AIDS: The Second Decade* (National Catholic AIDS Network, Inc., and Communications Ministry, Inc., 1995); 'NURTURING THE GIFT: gay and lesbian persons in seminary and religious formation', *CMI Journal*, **11** (Autumn 1988); 'Ministry with those suffering from HIV/Aids', a statement by Auxiliary Bishop John Ricard of Baltimore in *Origins*, **24** (26) (8 December 1994); and William D. Lindsey, 'The AIDS crisis and the Church: a time to heal', referred to earlier.

34   Smith, *AIDS, Gays, and the American Catholic Church*, p. 16.

35   Seubert, 'The sacramentality of metaphors', *Cross Currents* (Spring 1991), pp. 64–5.

36   *Ibid.*, p. 66.

5

Scripture in gay spirituality

Resources for the spiritual life

The gay person has the same resources for leading the spiritual life as has any other person, in particular, any other Christian. There can be no discrimination here. These resources are many but usually they include the Scriptures since they are the foundational documents of the Church. Secondly, the main theological teachings of Christianity are an important source since they provide the images by which the person relates to both God and community. The third main source is in various spiritual practices, often called asceticism.[1] These practices usually spring from a particular school of spirituality such as Franciscan or Ignatian. Here I would add that the more contemporary approaches to spirituality are relevant. For instance, creationist spirituality is widely known and also the system of the enneagram is being applied to the spiritual life in sometimes very creative and effective ways. The spiritual life would remain an abstraction without some form of spiritual exercises. Individual gay persons might follow more specific forms of the Christian tradition but whatever the school of spirituality, whatever the particular emphasis, these three main resources will usually be present in some way with varying degrees of emphasis.

Another way to approach the resources for Christian spirituality is to examine what Walter H. Principe calls the three levels of spirituality. For him these are first, the real or existential level of lived experience, second, the spirituality of groups and varying spiritual traditions, and third, the study of spirituality.[2] The latter or third level is not relevant here as it refers to the academic or practical study of spirituality as such. But the first two levels are related to the three resources that I mentioned above.

The most basic level of the lived experience for the Christian is very closely tied to the Scriptures which articulate the Christian life in terms of being led by the Spirit of God to become brothers and sisters in Christ. St Paul makes the distinction between the carnal and the spiritual person. We must avoid a superficial understanding of these terms. Spiritual for him means that the person's whole life is under the influence of the Spirit of God whereas the carnal person is one who is governed by that which is opposed to spirit. Paul does not oppose the material (body with its senses, for example) with the immaterial (the soul as understood in the theology from the Middle Ages until the time of the Second Vatican Council), but spiritual and carnal are two ways of living and being.[3] In that sense, my 'soul' could be both spiritual and carnal.

Principe's words call attention to two other very important aspects of the Christian spiritual life: one, that it must be inculturated,[4] and second, that it must culminate in dealing with issues of social justice. Principe's second level of spirituality, that of the spirituality of groups and differing spiritual traditions, emphasizes that although spirituality is personal, it is also received in a tradition. In other words, it is community formed and orientated. Any consideration of the liturgy presupposes that. The person is introduced into an inculturated spirituality. As he says:

> Hence a second level of Christian spirituality is that of a group, the family in the first instance and often the parish, but also for many the spirituality of a specialized group, e.g. (here he mentions the different denominations, religious communities, lay communities and movements such as the cursillo and charismatic groups).[5]

This second level is lived out in community liturgy, the guidance offered by different communities and the example of holy people. But much of the spirituality of groups has its origin in the Scriptures. The varying recognizable schools of spirituality emphasize a particular strand of New Testament spirituality, for example, Mark's kingdom of God or Matthew's Sermon on the Mount. Many find the strong sacramental character of John's Gospel attractive. All Christian spiritualities model themselves on the gospel but since they emphasize different aspects, considerable variety has developed. Some of the major contrasts are Eastern and Western, and Protestant and Catholic, and there are variations in each of these. All the sources of the spiritual life find their roots in the Scriptures to some degree and so we begin there. Liturgy will be treated in the next chapter and asceticism, spiritual practices and inculturation will be touched on in some of the other chapters. We have already referred to the area of social justice in a gay spirituality. We have also dealt with the teachings of the churches, albeit in a very narrow sense as the treatment did not move beyond the position of the churches on homosexuality.

The Christian Scriptures

That which many Christians find to be their most accessible as well as the most practical way to follow the spiritual journey, namely, reflection and prayer centred around the Bible, has become for many gays a barrier. The reason is obvious. The Bible has been used to accuse them before God and their neighbour of sinful behaviour. It has been employed as a justification for discrimination against them.[6] Those written witnesses of faith which most people find uplifting have become for many gays a form of diminishment and condemnation. Recently, in a course on the theology of relationships I assigned a gay novel to the class. I also showed them a well-produced and finely acted English movie, *The Lost Language of Cranes*. The written assignment was to assess a real gay, permanent and monogamous relationship which I described in some detail. Of the students who opposed the relationship (while admitting its humanizing qualities), most said it was condemned by the Bible. But they said no more than that. The so-called biblical principle that they were invoking was of the same level as a bumper sticker. Too often people condemn homosexuality with little more evidence than a *perception* of what they think the Bible says.

The irony is that the growing biblical scholarship today shows that the Bible says very little about homosexuality. It would be impossible to come up with a biblical position out of the few scattered references to same-sex experiences.[7] It is not clear that the Bible ever condemns homosexuality as we understand it since it is always mentioned in contexts where there is another overriding concern such as hospitality or ritual purity. Even those who conclude that the Bible does in fact condemn homosexuality do not claim that the Scriptures ever envisioned a gay, monogamous relationship in the way we tend to describe the gay relationship today. It is not necessary to find specific passages in Scriptures to be able to evaluate 'one night stands', male prostitution, and bathroom and bathhouse encounters as not promotive of life in God. Manipulative sex falls under the same judgement as any other kind of exploitation. But regarding two men or women in a committed loving relationship who truly do want to be together and want to give themselves to each other with as complete a vulnerability as possible, both the Bible and Jesus himself are silent.[8] Still the problem remains because popular perspective on homosexuality has not caught up with the developments in Scripture and the research in the human sciences.[9]

The Bible is being misused to marginalize and humiliate gay persons, to make them feel less than human, as if gayness is their fault, something that they decided one day that they wanted to have. The Scriptures are also used by sensitive intelligent Christians who believe that discrimination against gays is wrong, that they have the right to their dignity as anyone else, that they are no less loved by God than those who are straight. But they do not find in the Scriptures anything which would justify a place for homosexuality in the Christian tradition. Rather, they see in the Scriptures reasons why the gay person must remain celibate in order to be in right order with God and in good standing in the Church. There has been considerable tension in the churches over this matter as already indicated in an earlier chapter. Recently, the Presbyterian Church in the United States has voted to make its ban on the ordination of gays and lesbians part of their church law. Their Book of Order will now have the wording which will require chastity of its single ministers.[10] "'It says to the country that Presbyterians are committed to reaffirming their biblical center for faith and practice", said the Revd Jack Haberer of Houston, moderator of the Presbyterian Coalition, a group favouring the amendment.'[11] Clearly, people of good will and people who promote human understanding and greater social justice cannot find in the Bible that which would allow them to embrace the homosexual life-style as in accord with the Christian message.[12]

Where, then, does this kind of ambiguity leave the spiritual director, the directee and anyone who seeks spiritual nourishment in the Scriptures but who is unwilling to set aside his/her sexuality in his relating with God? The most important thing for director and directee to realize is that it is not possible to develop a spirituality of homosexuality out of a few references in the Bible any more than it is possible to develop a biblical position which would condemn the contemporary monogamous same-sex union. It is all of the Bible, taken as a whole, which is for gays a source of meditation, encouragement and exhortation. The Bible is no less a treasury for them than for anyone else. The only relevance that the few passages about homosexuality have for the gay person is the need to understand them so that they do not become a barrier in their being able to find nurture and comfort in the Scriptures. To have a clear notion of how these isolated passages function in the Bible will release the gay person to engage the Scriptures fully. It is also important for the directors to have a nuanced understanding of what the Bible says about homosexuality lest they try to relate to the directee from a prejudicial position. Both need to be freed from a kind of fundamentalism which has entered into the application of the Scriptures in the issue of homosexuality if together they are to make the imaginative journeys through the biblical stories which are so much a part of developing the spiritual life in the Christian tradition.[13] Directors might well note the comments of David Leal, professor of philosophy at Oxford University, speaking about biblical fundamentalism in the matter of homosexuality.

> It is important to be reminded that 'traditionalists' in this debate are not the only parties to be guilty of claims to own the truth. Yet the attitudes of some parties to Scripture lead to the conclusion that ownership of the truth is precisely the issue which most concerns this side of the debate as well. There are, of course, certain standard passages cited in relation to discussions of homosexuality, and the interpretation of most of them is to some extent controversial. It is undoubtedly tempting for those who feel confident in the truth of their cause to assert the meaning of these passages without undergoing the hard exegetical craft involved. They then find such an assurance of the truth of their interpretation that they appear to bypass the business of confrontation with the actual text altogether.[14]

I suggest that both director and directee begin with clearing away the kind of blindness that comes from lack of information. For those who wish to do the minimum amount of clarifying reading, I recommend the essay, 'What does the Bible say about homosexuality?', by Victor Paul Furnish.[15] He makes it clear that we cannot get answers from the Bible for questions it was not asking. 'There is nothing about sexual identity, sexual orientation, or the like. When one forces the Bible to address questions of which it has no conception, whatever answers one may get are not really *biblical* answers at all.'[16] Furnish says that to concentrate on a biblical teaching on homosexuality is to distract one from the Bible's agenda. It has far more to say about greed, self-interest, injustice in the marketplace, and exploitation of the poor than it does about sex with a person of the same sex. He notes that the various moral teachings in the Bible are an expression of concern that people be faithful to the claim that God makes on them. But because these rules and counsels are historically conditioned they may be less relevant for our time.[17] He presents a helpful survey of the passages which are most often discussed in the area of homosexuality.

I do not intend to review in any detail these various scriptural texts. This is not the place to do so. Hopefully, most directors and directees who have a concern that these passages are inhibiting a full engagement with the Scriptures will together spend some time reviewing them in the light of contemporary biblical scholarship. For those who wish to do a bit more in this study I recommend Daniel Helminiak's fine work, *What the Bible* Really *Says About Homosexuality*.[18] Dr Helminiak brings to the discussion considerable scholarship as well as a fine sensitivity to the issues shaped by his own experiences. He writes in a non-technical style making the biblical exegesis regarding the usual selected scriptural passages available to those who are not familiar with biblical studies. His conclusion is that

> the Bible supplies no real basis for the condemnation of homo-sexuality . . . Therefore, people must stop opposing homosexuality merely by quoting the Bible, because, taken on its own terms, the Bible simply does not support their case. If they have some other reason for their opposition, they ought to get clear what that reason is and state it up front.[19]

I would recommend his chapter on interpreting the Bible to any beginner and anyone tempted by the easy clarity of fundamentalism.[20] For many gays and lesbians who are troubled about the Bible and their life-style and/or sexual orientation it can be freeing to hear these words:

> The sin of Sodom was inhospitality, not homosexuality. Jude condemns sex with angels, not sex between two men. Not a single Bible text clearly refers to lesbian sex. And from the Bible's positive teaching about homosexuality, there follows no valid conclusion whatsoever about homosexuality . . . Indeed, the Bible's longest treatment of the matter, in Romans, suggests that in themselves homogenital acts have no ethical significance, whatsoever. However,

understood in their historical context, the teaching of 1 Corinthians and 1 Timothy, makes this clear: the abuse forms of male–male sex – and of male–female sex – must be avoided.[21]

It is important to note for the sake of balance that Helminiak does not find that the Bible is irrelevant for the spiritual life of gays and lesbians. It is not as if they are totally free to live sexually in any way that they wish. Those gays and lesbians who live by the Bible will follow it with the same discipline and self-control as do all who seek to adhere to Christ and his message.

I suggest that far from the Bible being an obstacle to the prayer life of gay persons, it can be the least problematic of the traditional resources available to them.[22] Stephen C. Barton has written an essay, which I would recommend to any gay person for whom Scripture is important, where he asks the question: 'Is the Bible good news for human sexuality? Reflections on method in biblical interpretation'. He begins this way: 'I wish to suggest that it is not the Bible that should be the main bone of contention. Rather, the focus ought to be on the readers: who it is who is reading the Bible and what it might mean for us to read the Bible well and wisely.'[23] His point is that we cannot use the Bible as a source of *information*. That is what the fundamentalist does in searching out appropriate proof texts to support some already entrenched position. The liberal historical critics also treat Scripture as a source of information when they try to ascertain the plain sense of the text. Barton puts it another way:

What if interpreting the Bible is not understood in these decidedly positivist terms as a kind of archaeological dig for historical facts or revelatory propositions? What if the Bible is more like the text of a Shakespearean play or the score of a Beethoven symphony, where true interpretation involves corporate performance and practical enactment, and where the meaning of the text or score will vary to some degree from one performance to another depending on the identity of the performers and the circumstances of the performance? . . . Its advantage is that it brings the reading of the Bible back into the process of community formation, celebration and mission, and places responsibilities on the community to read the texts in ways which are transforming and life-giving.[24]

This is an attractive analogy because it means that the director becomes a kind of orchestral conductor and play director who deals with his/her directees with different interpretations depending upon whether they are gay or straight, what differing experiences each brings to direction, and what relationships they have to the world around them. The good director will attend to such things as: is this gay man or women in a relationship? How long? What is understood by commitment? What is going on in the theological world regarding the place of homosexuality in the Christian tradition? All these elements must be brought into play as the director helps gay persons interpret the performance of their lives at this time. In working with the person over a period of time the director will change the interpretation depending on the growth of the individual in the life of prayer, commitment to others, involvement in social justice issues and the like. Simply telling his players (the directees) that homosexuality is wrong, so they must stop it, or to repeat what s/he said five years previously would make for a bad and boring play. Every gay man or lesbian in direction needs a kind of artistic director to help them move beyond the text (in this case, simplistic interpretations of Scripture or not very well nuanced statements from ecclesiastical authorities). Matters of gender and sexuality cannot be reduced to exegesis or eisegesis. We must always keep in mind the larger agenda of the Bible which cannot be made equivalent to what one does with one's genitals.

Barton warns against manipulating the Bible. This can be done by all sides. Fundamentalists do it in grossly obvious ways, but feminists do it and gays and lesbians can also make the Bible become the scapegoat for their anxieties. However, to move to an antiseptic neutral ground is no solution.[25] For this reason Barton says that we must start in some other place besides that of exegetical inquiry. We do not ignore exegesis. We just ask different questions: 'What is our experience as men and women in the Church and society today? And, what kind of people do we need to be in order to interpret wisely what the Bible says, in the way which is life-giving in the realms of gender and sexuality?'[26] After all, spiritual direction, like all forms of Christian ministry, is another way of proclaiming the gospel. When the director becomes artistic director, then the Bible can be good news for gay people. In our work of direction we must be people who know how to read the Bible in a life-giving and freeing way. This presupposes that the director who has been transformed by Christ in the tradition can best direct this play of which his/her directees are the players. I know from my own experience that a session in spiritual direction can have a cathartic effect no less significant than that which can come from a creatively interpreted play or an imaginatively recreated symphony. Together, director and directee can *perform* the Scriptures.

Biblical scholar, Timothy Luke Johnson, deals with the same issue when he addresses the matter of the hermeneutics of homosexuality, that is, how we interpret certain biblical texts which many believe refer to homosexuality. He puts it in the context of another major turning-point in the Christian community's history, namely, the spread of the gospel to the Gentiles. Stressing the importance of table fellowship in New Testament times, Johnson notes that early Christians had to reread their tradition to allow non-Jews to become Christians without observing the legal requirements of the Torah. It was an agonizing and difficult task for 'that first generation of Christians to allow their perception of God's activity to change their perceptions, and use that new experience as a basis for reinterpreting scriptures'.[27] For the Church to recognize the possibility of a gay, committed, monogamous and lifelong relationship would be similar to what the Church faced in early Christianity in admitting Gentiles into the community.[28] They made their decision to admit Gentiles without requiring Jewish law based on their listening to what God was doing in the life of the Gentiles. Johnson says:

> On the basis of this experience of God's work, the church made bold to reinterpret Torah, finding there unexpected legitimation for its fidelity to God's surprising ways . . . (The church) is called to discern the work of God in human lives and adapt its self-understanding in response to the work of God. Inclusivity must follow from evidence of holiness: are there narratives of homosexual holiness to which we must begin to listen?[29]

I would be remiss, even dishonest, if I gave the impression that the above is the only possible way to deal with the Scriptures in the matters of homosexuality. The director who is Roman Catholic and is dealing with a Roman Catholic[30] would be wise to acquaint him/herself with a different view, one which is also relevant to the directee. The resource here that I suggest is Gerald D. Coleman SS, *Homosexuality: Catholic Teaching and Pastoral Practice*.[31] Readers will find here what they would expect: a clear statement of the official position of the Catholic Church regarding the morality of homosexual genital acts. This is a position widely known, even by those who have little to do with organized religion. Coleman is faithful to the Church's teaching and gives a clear presentation of it.[32] He is also genuinely concerned about real people who happen to be gays and lesbians. Therefore, this is not just a book on moral theology but one on pastoral care as well.

Coleman discusses the usual scriptural texts long associated with homosexuality in the Bible, e.g. Genesis 19:1–11; Leviticus 18:21b–23 and 20:13; 1 Corinthians 6:9–11; 1 Timothy 1:8–11; Romans 1:22–7. As the reader might suspect, Coleman's understanding of these passages differs from much of the understanding of biblical scholars who comment on these texts. For instance, he disagrees with the interpretation of the destruction of the city of Sodom made by John Boswell, who claims that we are not dealing here with sexuality as such, namely, anal intercourse, but with the inhospitable treatment of visitors.[33] Coleman ends his treatment of the Genesis 19 text (the Sodom and Gomorrah story): 'Boswell concludes, "There is no sexual interest of any sort in the incident." Such an interpretation is erroneous and should sustain no credibility.'[34] The same kind of disagreement with Boswell is found also regarding some of the other passages. I feel certain that Coleman would distinctly reject the conclusion arrived at by Robin Scroggs in his *The New Testament and Homosexuality*:

> The *fact* remains, however, that the basic model in today's Christian homosexual community is so different from the model attacked by the New Testament that the criterion of reasonable similarity of context is not met. The conclusion I have to draw seems inevitable: *Biblical judgments against homosexuality are not relevant to today's debate*. They should no longer be used in denominational discussions about homosexuality, should in no way be a weapon to justify refusal of ordination, *not because the Bible is not authoritative*, but simply because it does not address the issues involved.[35]

I sense that Coleman is not all that comfortable with his reading of the texts given the amount of sophisticated attention which has been given to them by biblical scholars. He is too honest to try to get the Bible to say things it did not say. And so his conclusion:

> It is important to affirm, then, the historical and human character of the Bible. At the same time, however, neither attribute describes the

Bible's final reality. It is only when we recognize the Bible as the word of God and the book of the church that we name its full and intended reality.[36]

Few directees would care to get into the intricacies of the meaning of certain Greek words, the intention of the author and the originating context of so few passages in Scripture. To do so would be a distortion of the Bible as a resource for the spiritual life. For the directee for whom all of this is irrelevant, it should remain so and the director would be unwise to introduce biblical interpretation explicitly. In my many years of counselling gay and lesbian persons rarely have I found that matters of an exegetical nature came up. Their concerns are not along those lines. Unfortunately, it sometimes means that the Scriptures do not play an important part in their spiritual lives. If the director encourages them to move more into the biblical material, s/he should be prepared for the fact that some of these passages may become problematic.

A director who has more than the rare gay directee would find it very useful to do some in-depth reading in this area of biblical interpretation. In particular I would recommend *Homosexuality and Christian Community*, edited by Choon-Leong Seow. The contributors are members of the faculty from Princeton Theological Seminary. The volume is a result of the discussions going on in the Presbyterian Church regarding the ordination of gays and lesbians. This is a response to that discussion on the part of some faculty members. The collection of essays represents a wide perspective of views. These essays would be especially helpful for the director, gay or straight. What the editor of the book says about homosexuality will have been the experience of many heterosexual directors. It is worth quoting in full:

> I also used to believe that homosexual acts are always wrong. Listening to gay and lesbian students and friends, however, I have had to rethink my position and reread the scriptures. Seeing how gay and lesbian people suffer discrimination, face the rejection of family and friends, risk losing their jobs, and live in fear of being humiliated and bashed, I cannot see how anyone would prefer to live that way. I do not understand it all, but I am persuaded that it is not a matter of choice. Seeing how some gay and lesbian couples relate to one another in loving partnerships, observing how much joy they find in one another, and seeing that some of them are better parents

than most of us will ever be, I have reconsidered my views. I was wrong.[37]

Whatever an individual director might hold regarding the morality of homosexual acts, the attitude of openness and compassion in that statement is indispensable for doing spiritual direction with a gay person.

Several other essays in this collection deserve close reading by directors and directees who find that they have seemingly unresolvable questions when they approach the Bible, whether in the liturgy or private prayer. For some, Paul seems to be the greatest stumbling block. I recommend the essay by Brian K. Blount, 'Reading and understanding the New Testament on homosexuality', for a discussion on such issues of how homosexuality is not a fundamental part of Pauline teaching, how the ground has shifted in the reality that moved Paul to condemn homosexual activity. In helping one to pray the Scriptures it will not do simply to ignore the Pauline corpus lest we happen upon a text which we find embarrassing or unexplainable.

> We are, therefore, called not simply to read Paul into the twentieth century, but to understand him for, and in light of, the twentieth-century context. And if his own writings are to be any guide, of what God is doing ultimately through Jesus Christ, he does so in a way that brings radical newness and inclusion.[38]

Those of us who do spiritual direction with gay persons have the responsibility to be knowledgeable in this area of Scripture and homosexuality. This is not because our directees will be bombarding us about the meaning of individual scriptural passages. They almost never ask that. But rather that we may be free to deal with Scripture as a whole and lead the directee to find ways to live a biblical spirituality and to do so without reserve.[39] Gay Christians not only have the right to have the same power of the Bible released in them as do straight Christians, but there is no way they can maintain a Christian identity or draw upon their tradition creatively (even if they do not go to church) if these charter documents of Christianity play no part in their relationship with God. There is much there for them. Siker's closing words of his essay seem a fitting conclusion for this section:

> In conclusion, I would argue that the Bible does not give us clear guidelines regarding the inclusion of gays and lesbians in the

Christian community, but it does give us clear guidance regarding treatment of one another as God's wheat. It does provide clear directions regarding the inclusion of those who, even to our surprise, have received the Spirit of God and join us in our Christian confession . . . With Peter and Paul, are we up to the challenge of recognizing, perhaps with surprise and with humility, that gay and lesbian Christians, *as* gays and lesbians and not as sinners, have received the Spirit in faith? If so, let us welcome our newfound brothers and sisters in Christ and get on with the task to which God has called us all.[40]

Notes

1 The philosopher, Michel Foucault, wrote on asceticism in a way that other writers have found helpful for understanding asceticism in relation to homosexuality. See David M. Halperin, *Saint Foucault: Towards a Gay Hagiography* (Oxford: Oxford University Press, 1995).

2 See the article 'Spirituality, Christian', in Michael Downey (ed.), *The New Dictionary of Catholic Spirituality* (Collegeville, MN: The Liturgical Press, 1993), p. 932.

3 *Ibid.*, p. 931.

4 In his article, 'Culture', in *The New Dictionary of Christian Spirituality* (pp. 242–4), Darrell J. Fasching speaks of the inculturation of spirituality this way:

> We now live at a unique point in history, one that offers perhaps the greatest challenge yet to Christian spiritual patterns of life. We live in a time of the meeting of the world's religions in an emerging world culture. It is a time when Christian patterns of spirituality are encountering their counterparts in other religions. The spiritual adventure of our time, says theologian John Dunne, is one of 'passing over' into other religions and culture in order to 'come back' with new insight into our own.

5 Downey (ed.), 'Spirituality, Christian', p. 932.

6 See Chapter 3, 'Texts of terror', in Nancy Wilson, *Our Tribe: Queer Folks, God, Jesus, and the Bible* (HarperSanFrancisco, 1995). Wilson borrows the term, 'texts of terror', from the scripture scholar Phyllis Trible, who treats certain passages of Scripture which have been used to justify violence and discrimination of women. Wilson uses the same method regarding those texts in the Bible which have been used to justify homophobia in the Church and culture.

7 William De Lindsey notes: 'When one compares the few biblical texts that appear to deal with homosexuality with the wealth of texts forbidding practices we might now call capitalistic, one wonders even more at our contemporary allocation of weight to the "homosexual" texts, and our elision of the others.' See footnote 14 of his 'The AIDS crisis and the Church: a time to heal', in Adrian Thatcher and Elizabeth

Stuart (eds), *Christian Perspectives on Sexuality and Gender* (Grand Rapids, MI: Eerdmans, 1996), pp. 347–67.

8　What this means is that churches that do condemn homosexual relationships must draw upon more than biblical resources such as tradition or the natural law.

9　David Power, in an article dealing with the biblical evidence in the matter of the ordination of women, speaks of tradition itself as 'a constant process of inter-pretation . . . It is possible for a long time to merely quote standing texts found in Scripture, in magisterial documents, and in patristic and medieval writings, as long as no new questions have emerged. The scrutiny of tradition is however recast when the condition of an age in the life of the Church bring forth new issues and new questions.' See his 'Church order, the need for redress', *Worship*, **71** (4) (July 1997), pp. 291–309.

10　Presumably, this would refer to all single ministers whatever their sexual orientation. The gay person 'in the know' would want to make the counterclaim that their sexual relationship with their partner is in fact *chaste*. To be celibate is to be unmarried. To be chaste is to live a sexual life which is at the service of others. In the *Sexual Celibate* (New York: Seabury, 1974) Don Goergen says that the chaste person is one who 'places the intense pleasure associated with genital interaction at the service of love' (pp. 100–1).

11　As reported in the *San Antonio Express-News* (Wednesday 19 March 1997).

12　In the **OP-ED** section of the *New York Times* (5 April 1997) Bruce Bawer notes that Protestants are parting company on the issue of the ordination of practising gays. It is more a divide between north and south than between the denominations. He sees that there are two religions emerging in Protestantism, the church of law and the church of love. These two churches disagree on such things as Christian identity and, of course, the Bible. The battle over gay ordinations is simply one more conflict 'over the most fundamental questions of all: What is Christianity?' Bawer predicts that due to the difference in these two churches, 'the next generation will see a realignment in which historical denominations give way to new institutions that more truly reflect the split in American Protestantism'.

13　Again, David Power, in 'Church order', says, referring to Paul Ricoeur: 'As he proposes it, the canonical scriptures have an irreplaceable role in Christian tradition and community. However, the Church has never been able to give a rigidly immut-able interpretation of that text, simply because it never fully seizes its life-force. In the context of living the scriptural faith in the gift of the Spirit, communities are constantly interpreting it. They also join it to other texts, rites, institutions, and examples of living, setting it thus into what we broadly call tradition.'

14　David Leal, *Debating Homosexuality* (Cambridge: Grove Books, 1996), pp. 20–1.

15　Found in Sally B. Geis and Donald E. Messer (eds), *Caught in the Crossfire: Helping Christians Debate Homosexuality* (Nashville: Abingdon Press, 1994).

16　*Ibid.*, p. 58.

17　*Ibid.*, p. 63. I am not saying that, because it is not possible to develop from biblical sources a position on committed homosexual relationships as we understand them today, the churches which condemn them are wrong. I am concerned here that the director and directee treat the Bible on its own terms lest it become a stumbling-block in the spiritual growth of gays and lesbians.

18   David Helminiak, *What the Bible* Really *Says About Homosexuality* (San Francisco: Alamo Square Press, 1994). See also Michael Vasey, *Strangers and Friends: A New Exploration of Homosexuality and the Bible* (London: Hodder and Stoughton, 1995).

19   *Ibid.*, p. 14.

20   Fundamentalism's effect on homosexuality is not limited to the Scriptures. See the article by Stephen Mo Hanan, 'Knitting in public: on the common root of conservatism and homophobia', *White Crane*, 33 (Summer 1997), pp. 16ff. A fuller treatment of religious fundamentalism is found in Kathleen Ritter and Craig O'Neill, *Righteous Religion: Unmasking the Illusions of Fundamentalism and Authoritarian Catholicism* (New York: The Haworth Pastoral Press, 1996).

21   *Ibid.*, pp. 107–8.

22   With such a statement I am prescinding from the difficulties raised by the feminist critique of the Bible. These objections would also need to be resolved in many cases by director and gay directee, especially if the directee is lesbian.

23   Stephen C. Barton, 'Is the Bible good news for human sexuality?', in Thatcher and Stuart (eds), *Christian Perspectives on Sexuality and Gender*, pp. 4–13 (p. 4).

24   *Ibid.*, p. 6.

25   *Ibid.*, p. 7.

26   *Ibid.*, p. 10.

27   Timothy Luke Johnson, 'Debate and discernment: Scripture and the Spirit', *Commonweal* (January 1994), p. 11. Also relevant here would be Bruce Bawer's *A Place at the Table* and Nathan Mitchell's wonderfully insightful treatment of table fellowship in his 'Eucharist as sacrament of initiation', *Forum Essays*, 2 (Chicago: Liturgy Training Publications, 1994).

28   It is clear that certain communions do reject homosexual activity without condemning the orientation itself. The Roman Catholic Church is one of these. I take it that Johnson's point is the need to listen to the Spirit of God and that this Spirit is also found in the Church through gays and lesbians.

29   Johnson, 'Debate and discernment', p. 13.

30   As well as directors of other Christian traditions but who regularly give direction to Roman Catholics and others who adhere to a position on homo–genital acts similar to that of the Catholic Church.

31   Gerald D. Coleman SS, *Homosexuality: Catholic Teaching and Pastoral Practice* (New York: Paulist Press, 1995).

32   This does not mean that he represents the general thinking of Roman Catholic theologians. Many, if not most, would probably be more nuanced than Coleman on certain issues. Representing an official position of a church in exploring any issue, even when not as explosive as sexuality, creates a methodological problem. I remember quite well when I was a theological student at Woodstock College in Maryland (at that time, one of the best of theological schools) being asked the question in an examination: what is the task of the theologian? The expected (required?) answer was: to find in Scripture and the tradition support for what the Church already teaches. We would not consider that a responsible way of proceeding in other scholarly disciplines. I would presume that this is something which theologians like Coleman must struggle with in their work, especially in light of the changing nature of human expression in words that can never 'say it all and say it perfectly'.

33 John Boswell, *Christianity, Social Tolerance and Homosexuality* (Chicago: The University of Chicago Press, 1980), pp. 93–5.

34 Coleman, *Homosexuality*, p. 61. For a different view see David Yegerlehner, 'Genesis 19: taking the offensive', *Harvard Gay and Lesbian Review*, 3 (4) (Fall 1996), pp. 19ff.

35 Robin Scroggs, *The New Testament and Homosexuality* (Philadelphia: Fortress Press, 1983), p. 127.

36 Coleman, *Homosexuality*, p. 71.

37 Choon-Leong Seow, 'A heterotextual perspective', *Homosexuality and Christian Community* (Louisville, KY: Westminster/John Knox Press, 1996), p. 25.

38 Brian K. Blount, 'Reading and understanding the New Testament on homosexuality', in *Homosexuality and Christian Community*, p. 37.

39 Choon-Leong Seow, *op. cit.* For continuing and more advanced reflection on the Scriptures and the gay person, I would further recommend Robert L. Brawley (ed.), *Biblical Ethics and Homosexuality* (Louisville, KY: Westminster/John Knox Press, 1996). The value of books of essays like this one and the previously mentioned one is that the reader has the opportunity to review contemporary thinking from many sides and there is less likelihood of simply following one author's agenda. The article by Jeffrey S. Siker, 'Gentile wheat and homosexual Christians: New Testament directions for the heterosexual church' (pp. 137–51), is a good summary of the present thinking of those who give a positive interpretation of the Scriptures in the matter of homosexuality as well as of those who address the matter with pastoral sensitivity.

40 Siker, 'Gentile Wheat and Homosexual Christians', p. 150. Because the area of Scripture has been the most problematic for the meaning of homosexuality in the Christian Church, there has developed a respectful literature on the topic. Other publications besides those referred to in the text would include: John Horner, *Jonathan Loved David: Homosexuality in Biblical Times* (Philadelphia: Westminster Press, 1978), which considers all the references to homosexuality in the Bible; the periodical, *The Other Side* (1994), contains some articles on Scripture and homosexuality: Mark Olson, 'Untangling the web', pp. 16–20, and Hendrik Hart, 'Romans revisited', pp. 23–8. For those interested, Nancy Wilson uses Scripture to develop a 'queer theology' in her book, *Our Tribe; Queer Folks, God, Jesus, and the Bible* (HarperSanFrancisco, 1995). Robert McAfee Brown has a short article, 'Sexuality and homosexuality: a problem for the churches', in *HIV/AIDS: The Second Decade* (National Catholic AIDS Network Inc., and Communications Ministry, Inc., 1995), pp. 31–5. Several British authors have contributed to the discussion of the Bible and homosexuality. For two opposing positions see *The Homosexual Way – A Christian Option?* by David Field (Grove Booklet on Ethics No. 9) which presents the traditional view and *Evangelical Christians and Gay Rights* by Michael Vasey (Grove Ethical Studies No. 80) for a more liberal view. For the traditional view but seen in a larger and more pastoral context see *Homosexuality and the Bible* by Mark Bonnington and Bob Fyall (Grove Biblical Studies No. 1). All are published by Grove Books Ltd (Ridley Hall Road, Cambridge, CB3 9HU).

6

Liturgy and embodiment

Introduction

Apart from Scripture there is another source for the spiritual life on the level of lived experience and that is the liturgy of the Church. Principe puts it well:

> Christian life in the Spirit takes place in an ecclesial context, in which celebration of word and sacrament culminates in the Eucharist (here occur important variations in Catholic and Protestant spiritualities). At the same time this experiential level of Christian spirituality embraces the whole human person (body, soul, spirit), who is part of a constantly changing material created order (physical, plant, animal), who is a symbolizing, ritualizing being, who learns and uses language for communication and self-expression; a person who is both an individual and a member of society, who is *inculturated* in place and time and so is affected by his or her social and personal history; a person, finally, who is called to serve others in the social, political, and economic orders.[1]

There is much in this statement that refers to the spiritual life and to direction. Practising Christians are identified by their involvement with the symbols of a particular tradition. To lead the spiritual life is to live in and through the patterned symbolic activity which we call ritual. And the specific rituals which carry a tradition are called its liturgy. It is this liturgy which embodies the main theological teachings of the tradition. For instance, it makes these teaching available for the Christian. For this reason the liturgist, Aidan Kavanagh, calls the liturgy not merely a source for theology but 'the very condition of doing theology, of understanding the Word of God. A liturgical act *is* a theological act of the most all encompassing, integral, and foundational kind.'[2] For similar reasons I call the liturgy the Church's most basic form of spiritual direction.

The liturgy as the Church's form of spiritual direction

What has been said in the previous chapter about the Scriptures applies to the liturgy directly. The liturgy of the word should be a liberating experience for gays and lesbians. The other texts of the liturgy should be considered in the same light as the biblical material itself. All this is necessary so that the liturgy is no less accessible to the gay person than it is to any other person. The point here is how the Church's liturgy is also a form of spiritual direction, a spiritual mentor.

The image of liturgy as spiritual mentor is an old one, as old as the liturgy itself. We are more conscious of liturgy's mentoring quality today since mentoring itself has become a more significant part of our lives. The most recent discussions about mentoring have been taking place in women's and men's groups. There are studies on how women mentor each other, and Robert Bly and other leaders in the various men's groups emphasize the need for young men to be mentored by older ones in a culture where adolescents see few alternatives to joining gangs in their attempt to discover themselves and create some identity.

The experience of mentoring from a religious perspective has most concretely been found in the tradition of spiritual direction. Tad Dunne, in his book called *Spiritual Mentoring*, says:

> The mentor may be any person willing and able to provide the psychological insight, the moral advice, and especially the spiritual guidance to someone making a serious decision. So let it be understood that by 'spiritual mentor' I mean any spiritual companion whatsoever.[3]

Gay men and women, especially younger gays, need mentors too. Sometimes, there may be an older gay man or woman who can fulfil that function. Often, that is not possible. Sometimes, the spiritual director, gay or straight, must step in to mentor a younger gay person. It is quite possible that the director will be mentoring, in a somewhat different sense, the middle-aged and older gay person. Not every spiritual director will automatically be a mentor to the directee. Yet, it would often be difficult to distinguish the two roles. Perhaps we could say that in some director/directee relationships the aspect of friend or companion as an equal is stronger while in others it is more the aspect of mentor/mentee which is salient. While the integrity of the relationship must always be maintained through trust and the director must do nothing to contaminate the relationship, when the director is also the mentor s/he may need to pay more attention to not taking advantage of the mentee/directee.[4]

Tilden Edwards, in his book *Spiritual Friend: Reclaiming the Gift of Spiritual Direction*, sees spiritual direction as 'one color on a many colored coat of resources. It is meant to be a part of the whole way of life, not an isolated resource.'[5] The churches have many forms of authentic guidance, some more than others: the rites of reconciliation, the sacraments and liturgy, retreats, spiritual reading and Scripture, devotions and pastoral counselling. Edwards gives several reasons why there is a special need for a spiritual friend today: support in a time when a shared world-view has collapsed, the fact that education and the psychological helping professions are limited in their ability to deal with people's hunger for transcendence, the need to restore a balance to a social-activist emphasis, and a reawakening of an oral tradition of guidance which has been neglected in our dependence on books and scholarship.[6]

Still, it is unrealistic to think that the majority of the population will ever have the opportunity of an individual spiritual mentor. And even when that is possible, the liturgy is still to be part of the lives of the directees. Part of the task of contemporary liturgical renewal should be the recovery of the liturgy as the Church's form of spiritual direction which is available to all worshipping Christians. The question is: how does the liturgy have the qualities to be a form of spiritual direction? And what does that mean for the gay person?

Kenneth Leech, in his work *Soul Friend*, opts for the name of soul friend to describe the director, a friend of the soul and a guide on the way. But he does not accept that spiritual direction can be reduced to conversation between friends where each speaks from ignorance or incompetence. For him the director can be identified by several marks, marks which I believe the liturgy also possesses and which makes it possible for the liturgy to be a form of spiritual direction:[7]

1. The director is a person possessed by the Spirit, someone characterized by holiness of life and closeness to God. Surely, if the liturgy is not also possessed by the same spirit of holiness, our faith is in vain. It is not that the liturgy is holy according to some abstract, Platonic ideal, but rather that it celebrates the faith present in the worshippers who are in relationship with God. Because the liturgy is an outward expression of an interior reality it gives the worshippers the opportunity to touch the holy in the symbols of ritual. The liturgy is a way of doing theology, it is spirituality in concrete form. But often our liturgical experiences lack this sense of embodiment. Although the language of liturgical theology speaks of this embodiment, the actual rites are often celebrated in a disembodied way. The reluctance in regard to singing, the exchange of the peace, the use of gestures, and certainly liturgical dance and movement all point to this lack of comfortability with the body. Richard Cleaver asks why.

> But could it be that we are ashamed of bodily exercises in church because we are ashamed of our bodies? Could it be that we offer such strenuous bodily worship at a different altar, dedicated to Nautilus, because we believe our bodies are not good enough for the God of Abraham?[8]

Embodied worship offers gay persons the opportunity to reaffirm the goodness of their bodies in a way which is more existentially engaging than simple intellectual affirmation which is what they might receive in a direction session. Part of the homophobic mentality is to speak of the disgusting things these men and women do with their bodies. Liturgy offers the possibility for gay persons to feel more integrated because good liturgy gives people permission to be aware of what exists below the neck. It encourages the freedom of movement and so an acceptance of bodily feeling. The kiss of peace is a time not only for physical contact between the opposite sexes but between the same sex. Cleaver, a gay writer, observes that sometimes at Eucharists when everyone is being hugged as part of the kiss of peace, he receives only a handshake. I doubt that this goes unnoticed. It becomes a challenge to the worshippers. The presence of gay persons in the liturgy will help to make liturgy more embodied because it will expand what people consider to be appropriate touching in the liturgy. In the liturgy there can be no untouchables.

The phenomenon of AIDS has made gays even more untouchable, more separated, more unclean. The squeamishness of some communicants regarding the sharing of the common cup has been unjustly directed toward those who are known to have AIDS or are HIV positive. Unfortunately, as a result, some church-goers are uncomfortable with the presence of gay people at the liturgy even though they do not in fact carry the virus. The liturgy needs to challenge our presuppositions here such as: that only gay people get AIDS, that all gay people are HIV positive, and that the disease can be spread by sharing the cup. In fact, it is the one with the weak immune system who is more threatened by the spread of disease through this method.[9] Assisting the directee to find some good liturgical experiences where touch is fully accepted will do more than hours of talking about the goodness of the human body and the sexuality of the gay person. Sad to say, such liturgies will be difficult to locate. Perhaps, the male directee needs to look for something like a men's ritual group.[10]

Good ritual is an expression of spirituality. It is as much a spiritual practice as is meditation. If ritual is alive and engaging, it can be one of the ways a person can move toward wholeness and holiness. For gay persons it can be the antidote to so much of the denigration of their bodies that they feel and that they inherited from family, society and the Church.

> By gathering in community to engage in symbolic action we can open the door to discovering ourselves so that we might experience the full life that is ours to live: everything from the pleasures of life, that we were often taught to deny ourselves, to the sorrows of our humanity that we have sought to escape.[11]

2. The director is a person of experience, someone who has already trod the spiritual path to a considerable degree, someone who has struggled with their own conflicts, darkness and light. The celebration of the liturgy brings with it hundreds of years of tradition, the experience of the Christian community since its foundation, carrying in its prayers and structure the pattern of centuries of Christian living with its struggles and victories. Through the centuries the liturgy has been a primary liminal experience for so many, a place where they could live temporarily on the margins, freed from the oppressive structures of society and its institutions. Unfortunately, the liturgy has not always been that for gays

and lesbians who have found in their worship only an additional form of oppression. So, the presence of gay/lesbian people in the liturgy is as much a challenge to the liturgy as the liturgy is a source of spirituality for them. To accept gay persons in the celebration of the liturgy means that the worshippers must accept their own sexuality. The integration of our sexuality both in our personal growth as well as in our spiritual lives is difficult because it is not simply an individual matter. We are carried along by centuries of alienation of sexuality and of the body from the spiritual life. The split between sexuality and spirituality in Christianity is well known.[12]

> The consequences of this split, this breaking off of sexuality as sinful, are devastating to gay and non-gay alike. Having a core part of ourselves that we are taught to tightly fear, question, and control, creates a society that is out of touch with a primal force . . . We are wonderfully made! Yet we are told in church that part of our very selves is sinful. In order to be spiritual, we must deny our bodily needs, and, most especially, deny our sexual needs.[13]

Gay persons in the liturgy will be an ever present challenge to the Church to be true to itself. How can worshipping communities continue to marginalize gays, demanding, in effect, that they remain silent about their sexuality, and still claim that sacramental life is about inclusiveness? Sacramental worship is about the removal of any ambiguity about the presence of God in creation and human living, about placing all of creation in the story of God's love for the world and God's desire for its transformation. For it to be authentic, then, it cannot allow the gay worshipper to remain hidden or to fall into a kind of limbo existence. At the end of a liturgy gays should not be left wondering what their place in the Body of Christ is, whether they have a role to play, and to what degree they are worthy to participate.

It is true that the liturgical texts and forms have been marked through the centuries by the struggles, conflicts and even deaths that the community has suffered, especially in its ethnic/racial minority groups. It is also true that not all the groanings in the Christian community have found voice and tongue in the liturgy. The homosexual voice has been silenced. Women's voices have been silenced too, but at least there are women who are visible in the history of salvation, beginning with Mary herself. Are there any gay people in the Bible that are like the gay people you know, whether brother, father, cousin, friend or acquaintance? We know that the liturgy reflects and brings to expression the actual community that is celebrating. Because the community is silent about homosexuality, the liturgy remains mute and so a deficient symbol. Liturgies celebrated by gay/lesbian groups such as Dignity[14] have their value for the individuals, but because groups like Dignity are themselves marginalized, so are their liturgical celebrations. The public acceptance of gays and lesbians into the Christian community could be as traumatic as was Paul's acceptance of the Gentiles without the need of their becoming Jews first, a point made by Jeffrey Siker. But if this is not done, the Body of Christ will remain fractured.

> The Church must realize that shameful silence produces a distorted image of God, the body of Christ, and of oneself, a dysfunctional search for intimacy, and entrapment of ordination, and many times, a complete exit from the Church. The Church's act of silencing lesbians and gays is not a passive or benevolent act of love. In silencing the complete selfhood of gay/lesbian Christians, the Church obstructs their full participation in the body of Christ.[15]

3. The director is a person of learning, which does not mean a doctorate in Christian spirituality, but someone who knows the tradition including some knowledge of Scripture, is competent in one or other school of spirituality, and knows something about the various forms of prayer. The liturgy in some real sense is the tradition of the Church, it is where Scripture comes alive in its proclamation and it is the spiritual source for the various schools of spirituality in the Church. Not much more needs to be added to this point here since all that has already been stated in the previous chapter regarding the place of Scripture in the life of the gay person would apply here. Nevertheless, I would like to stress the matter of how gays and lesbians can image God since so many of our God images are taken from Scripture. I will let the authors of *Equal Rites* speak for me:

> Images that focus on God's presence with humanity, and even on God's vulnerability, may be especially appropriate for lesbian/gay-oriented worship. Power images such as Judge and Father that emphasize divine omnipotence can be problematic because they have been used to oppress lesbian and gay people. Depending on the

worship context, lesbians, gay men, and their supporters may respond well to such images as Gentle One, Justice Seeker, Giver of Hope, Compassionate One, Healer, Comforter, Companion, Creator, lover, Amazing Grace, Liberator, Risk Taker, and Friend of the Poor.[16]

4. The director is a person of discernment, a gift which has a certain intuitive quality about it, enabling the director to perceive the inner life of the directee. The liturgy too has this intuitive quality because it is primarily a symbolic experience. Our form of worship is that of the proverbial tip of the iceberg, most of which lies in the area of the unconscious where so many of life's decisions are already made. The most significant part of the liturgical experience remains invisible. Yet part of liturgy's task is to bring to expression that which is hidden in the depth of the human heart and express it in ritual form. This surely is a form of discernment, but it is only so if the external forms of worship remain in contact with the deeper unconscious sources where the energy of all symbols resides. The authors of *Equal Rites* have written on this point.

> Ritual is an integral part of life. It provides the actions and forms through which people meet, carry out social activities, celebrate, and commemorate. Whether the acts appear casual or dramatic, sacred or secular, they express a meaning and significance that extend beyond the particular event itself. Rituals, like myths, address the urge to comprehend human existence; the search for a marked pathway as one moves from one stage of life to the next; the need to establish secure and fulfilling relationships within the human community; and the longing to know one's part in the vast wonder and mystery of the cosmos.[17]

Liturgy can become a place where gay persons gather in community, whether it be with other gays or not, where they can experience the life-giving acceptance of others, where they are permitted to touch themselves deeply. Spiritual discernment needs a context. It does not exist by itself. For many a gay person it will be ritual which provides this context.

Good ritual brings people together, strengthening the ties that already bind them, and creating new ones where ties do not already exist. And so ritual is very much about intimacy. Symbolic action touches and reveals our deepest selves and when this is shared we have true intimacy.[18]

Here is a clear example of how the liturgy can be a form of spiritual direction for the gay directee. So much of direction time will deal with issues of intimacy, in particular with blocks to intimacy because of society or family upbringing, because of lack of societal support, past broken relationships, betrayal and abuse. The liturgy may offer gay men and women the chance for some self-nurturing, some contact with themselves as bodies needing the contact of other bodies, and a way of letting the unconscious express its desires and needs in symbolic forms.

The increasing interest in the formation of gay and lesbian ritual groups says that the need for ritual is no less present than in the past. It may be that a gay man or woman will find their most meaningful ritual experiences in these groups where the ritual is a way for them to discover their identity. As the writer, Robert Barzan, in the *White Crane Newsletter* put it: 'We are learning to drink from our own inner wells of refreshment, find there the direction and nourishment we need to continue the life journey.'[19] Gay ritual groups can help make it possible for gays to participate more fully in the Church's liturgy because now, already grounded ritually, they can bring resources to the liturgy as well as receive the particular Christian shape to their spiritual life. The Christian Church has had experience with ritual for a long time and can offer much to those men and women who are searching for resources in constructing their own rituals.[20] In any event, the director should encourage directees, gay or not, to use their imaginations in creating ritual experiences.[21] The authors of *Equal Rites* speak to the urgency of this matter.

Lesbians and gay men are in need of a greater ability, perhaps even a greater willingness, to live symbolically. They make the best they can of their circumstance without, for the most part, the benefit of inspiring myths and rituals that are attuned to the unique needs of sexual minorities. All lesbian and gay men have suffered the loss of positive self-images as a direct result of their second-class status and consequent objectification in a heterosexual-dominant society. It is painful to consider the countless lives wasted, the talents atrophied, and the sickness suffered by sexual minorities who were never allowed, much less encouraged, to know themselves and take strength and happiness in that knowledge. Rites play an important role in offering lesbians and gay men images and symbols that affirm their experience.[22]

5. The director is a person who gives way to the Holy Spirit. Christian spiritual direction is Christian because all is done in the context of faith in the power of the Spirit of God to move the individual to deeper union with God. Direction then is a means and not an end. 'The end is God, whose service is perfect freedom.'[23] It seems superfluous to comment on this last quality of the spiritual director as applying to the liturgy since it is a description of what liturgy is all about: living in a world of faith, under the guidance of the Spirit to achieve closer union with God as a community.

Union with God is a mature experience, one of great depth. It is not some kind of romantic outburst. The guidance of the liturgy can help gay directees (and any directee) to look at the place of romance in their lives. Is it something which is equated with sexual experience? Is it that which only turns gays more inward, making them more selfish, less aware of a world in need? The liturgy can help gay people to see that their union with God, while it might make use of sexual imagery, does not require the presence of sexual exchange in their lives. On the other hand, an embodied liturgy may make it possible for them to discover that union with God is found in their experience of their sexuality. Whatever form this homosexual experience takes for gay directees, the call of the liturgy will be to move away from a personal spiritual life which does not lead to greater sensitivity to the needs of the world around them. It can help them grasp that all of their relationships, especially their romantic ones, are part of a larger social structure. Union with God, union with others, and union in intimate friendship must move in the same direction, namely, the urging of human structures to become more fully human. This union with God cannot be separated from union with one's brothers and sisters, one's community wherever that may be found. John J. McNeill speaks to this:

> The whole meaning and direction of our spiritual growth is a movement from isolation and alienation into greater union with each other. At Holy Communion, each of us receives the body of Christ, and being one with the body of Christ, we shall become one with each other. This is a symbolic prophecy of the mysterious and joyous

transformation of our bodies at the resurrection, when our bodies will become the perfect means of communication and oneness.[24]

Union with God for the Christian must mean union with Christ and also with the Church.[25]

Perhaps, one of the most difficult tasks of spiritual direction will be to help the gay directee to 'take a chance on the church', to paraphrase the title of McNeill's book. To make this possible, it may be important for an individual gay directee to belong to some form of the gay community such as a gay support group or a gay ritual group. It is important that the gay man or woman experience the positive support from a community, however loosely connected with the Church, to counteract some of the negative messages coming from the official Church. The reasons that McNeill gives for the importance of the gay community for the gay person apply particularly to the gay directee. Gathering together in real celebrating communities, gay men and women can find their personal dignity upon which they can build a life based on the 'dignity' of the daughters and sons of God. Gays who approach direction in a wounded fashion because of the alienation, silence and separation imposed on them, need some help in self-acceptance. The acceptance in these gay groups provides the groundwork for their acceptance of themselves in the Church where the response to them may be ambiguous. McNeill points out that not only has this been the first time in history where there existed anything like a Christian gay community where gays can seek support as they try to integrate their sexuality in their spiritual lives, but

> the impact of the gay Christian community on the American church has been powerful. There is no question that most churchgoers are much more aware of the existence and the problems of gay Christians and take a more open, pastoral attitude toward them than was the case in the past.[26]

Not only does the liturgy presuppose community, it must presuppose the gay community as well.

The place of the liturgy in the spiritual life of the gay person is expressed eloquently by Cleaver:

> In the liturgy, we break the Word and we break bread, but breaking is not why we come. We perform these ritual acts to recreate the body

of Christ and to become one people of God around the table. Just so, gay men are not creating our theology to break the body of Christ. We break the Word of God open so that we can see into its depths. We break bread together to be united to one another. We will raise our voices in song and in prayer, just as we always have; what will be different is that we will use our real voices and call out our real names. The body is damaged not when our presence around the table is acknowledged but when it is forbidden.[27]

For gay Christians in particular, liturgical worship must 'become the paradigm of the breaking down of all human division and inequality'.[28] Liturgists speak of liturgy as a kind of play, playing at the kingdom of God. It is an hour-long, once-a-week rehearsal for this kingdom where we act as if all that Christ desired for this world has come about. It is a dress rehearsal for the actual experience of our world made complete. This is not merely poetic imagery. It implies that for this hour the usual barriers that dominate our lives, in particular our sexual dualism, become irrelevant. True, these barriers return once we leave our worship. But hopefully, they will have less control over our lives. Liturgy will not automatically change a homophobic society into one which accepts homosexuality as a gift; however, liturgy can assist the process because it serves a prophetic role. In another place I described that prophetic role thus:

> Establishing the kingdom of God is not primarily a dramatic happening. It must also take the form of justice to oneself, that is, of self-acceptance and deep contact with one's bodily self. The liturgy can be a most appropriate place to experience the justice in one-self, namely, that one is loveable and loved. Worship does not supply the solutions for removing the injustices of society. It offers no recipes for how to deal with international conflict, debilitating family structures, or social tensions . . . it is worship which makes possible this process whereby the worshippers can get in touch with fundamental experiences of justice, or lack of them. From such insight they can move to action in building this kingdom.[29]

I do not naively believe that most Sunday services are this kind of liturgy for gays or anyone else. Gays and lesbians are called to find liturgical services or to create their own ritual experiences where they can have a place where they can communally discern forms of injustice so as to move to greater liberation. Here they will experience their true liminality. Here the sexually dispossessed take possession of their sexuality. Here the sexually poor become sexually rich. Hopefully, even now some gay men and women will be able to find in the Church's liturgy the place where they can reclaim the goodness of their fully sexual bodies. Part of the ministry of spiritual direction will be to make Christian liturgy a place where all divisions become irrelevant, especially the division between body and spirit.

Sacramental touch in spiritual direction

It is appropriate to discuss the place of touch in spiritual direction in the context of liturgy where the body and touch are constantly affirmed in the sacramental rites. There is no rite in which we do not touch. When touch is done in a ritualized form and when it is accompanied by prayers and done in a context of faith it conveys and acknowledges the value of the embodied person. To touch someone in a religious rite is to place in a faith context the action of the human hand as it is experienced outside of ritual, such as in the medical world. Sacramental touch is not mere physical touch, any more than sickness is something confined purely to medical categories.

Touch has its place in spiritual direction, either in the sessions themselves or in a different professional context. Some may find this shocking. Certainly, some directors would be as adamant about the avoidance of any touch as are good therapists. This is understandable given the litigious nature of society today. But we must also acknowledge that now it is not unusual at a retreat house or during a retreat to have a professional person who does massage or different kinds of body work, precisely as a spiritual practice. The response to these people has been good. They work in a context of prayer and great respect for the person. I am not suggesting that spiritual directors touch their directees so much as that they recommend some form of body-work, including self-touch, to those directees whom they judge would profit from it.

Touch is the medium of human relationships and healing. Through the human body the person touching and the person being touched are able to identify with each other as well as separate as individual persons. Touch serves as a bridge of connection, especially in the case of separation, psychological and spiritual as well as physical. Touch can be a significant factor in dealing with the separation and alienation that gay women and men feel from society, family and Church because it is precisely their sexual bodies which are isolated whether from themselves or others. I do not believe that the reintegration of their bodies can be done through mental and verbal processes only.

To touch someone, one must know how to touch. One must touch with the whole self and not only with the hands. Just as integration implies that the entire self is delivered in physical communication, so the laying on of hands of the person touching must imply the total presence of that person. In other words, if we wish to touch others, we must first be able to touch ourselves. For unless we are the recipients of our own touch ministry, we cannot extend that ministry to others.

This is not a general endorsement of the use of touch in spiritual direction. Touch should only take place under the most professional of all conditions. The trust level between director and directee must have reached a high level. The director him/herself must have not only a degree of comfortableness in this matter but also have some competence in what generally can be called body-work.[30] Many directors would not be at home with the use of touch. When they discern that the person could be helped by some body-work they can refer that person to a professional.[31] It is probably the exception that the body-work is done in a direction session itself. There are many practices that the director can recommend which directees can do on their own. Tai Chi is one of the most obvious.[32]

The integration of the spiritual and physical is at the heart of the spiritual practice of touching the human body. For instance, the use of touch in something like spiritual direction can serve to assist the person to greater contact with their feeling level so as to enable them to experience their bodies freed from locked-in emotions. This may also lead to the radiance of the body where the psychic energy flows and directs the body's movement in this world. While busy executives might seek out a masseur or masseuse to calm themselves after a hectic day of watching the stock market rise and tumble, the person using massage to deepen their relationship with God will seek out someone whose own personal resources are sufficiently integrated and mobilized on behalf of others. I have found that both gays and straights have profited from the experience of touch of differing kinds both inside and outside direction. The more holistic experience of the coming together of the material and spiritual aspects of the self, the growing ease of touching and seeing one's body as well as being touched and being seen, and the deepening appreciation of the self as a creature of God with its own beauty are results that gays and straights share in common.[33] But I think gays have a special need to be touched because there is so much about themselves, both their bodies as well as their very persons, which do not receive the kind of daily affirmation that straights get. Because so many gay people carry in their very skin and tissues a kind of self-hatred, a shame of their sexual desires, and the kind of alienation from family, society and church which leads to alienation from God, I believe they need to explore seriously this path of healing. And for those on the spiritual journey I consider it almost indispensable.

As there are qualifications for anyone to be a masseur or masseuse, so there are for the art of bodily anointing. Those qualify who, in their touching of others communicate their own powerful psychic energies to their clients, activating in them their natural sources of healing and nourishment. The interaction between the professional and the client may have the usual soothing and comforting, indeed exhilarating qualities of secular massage, but the proper effect of this kind of anointing work is to place them in an attitude of contemplation where they experience the dissolution of the division of body and spirit. This non-verbal experience will help them to think about the deeper issues of existence. It will enable them to have an experience of what the liturgy is about as an anticipation of a world where division and dualism has ceased. This is more than what is often called body-work.[34] There is no aspect of the human personality that can be bypassed in this more spiritual process. What is sought is the harmonious balance of the personality which can serve as an image of a balanced world made up of people of so many different backgrounds, temperaments and insights working and acting as an integrated body in union with creation itself. When gay directees feel in the very tissues of their body this harmony, it is at such a moment that their bodies become sacraments.

Embodied worship, then, does for gays and lesbians what it does for heterosexuals. It is the usual, more accessible form of spiritual direction. It opens up the liturgy itself so that its own power is released in the worshipper. And it does what all good spiritual direction does, namely, it moves us beyond our more narcissistic concerns with our own personal bodies to the experience of being the body of Christ. Our individual bodies with all their limitations are incorporated into this larger body of Christ. This more social and empowering bodiliness we acquire through this inclusion means that our own bodies can move beyond the confines of our skin and extend to the spheres of influence our individual lives create. For gays and lesbians this means that they are not alone, that they contribute no less than others to the whole Christ, and that they can make their unique contribution both 'in filling up what is lacking in the sufferings of Christ' as well as in helping to create that 'divine milieu' in which we all need to live and grow.

Notes

1   Walter H. Principe, 'Christian spirituality', in Michael Downey (ed.), *The New Dictionary of Catholic Spirituality* (Collegeville, MN: The Liturgical Press, 1993), p. 932 (emphasis added).

2   Aidan Kavanagh, *On Liturgical Theology* (New York: Pueblo Publishing, 1984), p. 89. He calls the liturgy primary theology. Secondary theology is what most people think theology is.

3   Tad Dunne, *Spiritual Mentoring* (San Francisco: Harper, 1991), p. xiv.

4   Adolf Guggenbuehl-Craig, *Power in the Helping Professions* (Dallas: Spring Publications, Inc., 1982, latest printing), is still a wonderful guide for the director.

5   Tilden Edwards, *Spiritual Friend: Reclaiming the Gift of Spiritual Direction* (New York: Paulist Press, 1980), see Chapter 4.

6   *Ibid.*, pp. 99–102.

7   See Kenneth Leech, *Soul Friend* (San Francisco: Harper and Row, 1977), pp. 88 and 89 for a description of these qualities.

8   Richard Cleaver, *Know My Name: A Gay Liberation Theology* (Louisville, KY: Westminster/John Knox Press, 1995), p. 115.

9   We must note that the spread of disease through the common cup is not well established, if at all. Nevertheless, it would not be unusual in a Roman Catholic parish where almost everyone goes to communion to find that only 50 per cent receive from the cup. People refrain for many reasons: devotion, health, aesthetics. There are many places in the liturgy where the uncomfortableness with our bodies is manifested: embarrassment regarding liturgical movement, the kiss of peace, and receiving from the common cup.

10 Ironically, there may actually be more embodied liturgies available for those directees who are not Christian or who have moved away from the mainline denominations. Metropolitan Congregational Churches might provide some nurturing experiences for these. Also, there are many places where a kind of non-confessional ritual takes place. Some of these are a form of secular rituals; others have their roots in religious expressions such as that of the Native American. Mature directees might take advantage of some of these as long as they experience no conflict with their main religious commitment.

11 From the article, 'Gay rites primer', which appeared in *The White Crane Newsletter: For the Development of Gay Men's Spirituality* (P.O. Box 170152, San Francisco, CA 94117–0152, Summer 1990), p. 1.

12 For a treatment of the ambivalence toward sexuality in the history of Western culture and how that has been concretized in the area of homosexuality see Jamke Highwater, *The Mythology of Transgression: Homosexuality as a Metaphor* (New York: Oxford University Press, 1997). Highwater's book is a study of outsiders (homosexuals being one example) and how they have had a profound influence upon the culture at large. He 'points to a paradox at the center of Western values – the competing notions that the outsider is at once sinful and wise, that in everyday life the transgressor is ostracized, while in our most durable folklore and religious legends, heroes must break the rules to achieve greatness' (from book jacket). For him homosexuality is our modern metaphor of transgression. He provides much food for reflection on why we are so conflicted and contradictory about such an important and so natural a part of our lives. His work helps to explain why in Christian liturgy we use sexual imagery and even sexual (at least very sensual) gestures and yet are so hesitant to acknowledge sexuality as an indispensable part of our journey to God.

13 Marilyn Bennet Alexander and James Preston, *We Were Baptized Too: Claiming God's Grace for Lesbians and Gays* (Louisville, KY: Westminster/John Knox Press, 1996), p. 54. This is a good book for dealing with the place of the sacraments in the spiritual life of gays.

14 Dignity is the American national organization of Roman Catholic homosexuals which promotes various causes in support of gay people and provides a home for many Catholic gays. There are many local groups throughout the United States, who gather for their own liturgical celebrations. In many places they are not allowed to meet and celebrate liturgy in Catholic churches because they do not distance themselves from a position which is open to homoerotic genital activity among gays.

15 Alexander and Preston, *We Were Baptized Too*, p. 21.

16 Kittredge Cherry and Zalmon Sherwood, *Equal Rites: Lesbian and Gay Worship, Ceremonies, and Celebrations* (Louisville, KY: Westminster/John Knox Press, 1995), pp. xvi–xvii. I recommend that director and directee acquaint themselves with Larry Kent Graham, *Discovering Images of God: Narratives of Care among Lesbians and Gays* (Louisville, KY: Westminster/John Knox Press, 1997). See Chapter 8 for some discussion of the images of God and the liturgy.

17 Cherry and Sherwood, *Equal Rites*, p. xiii.

18 Robert Barzan, *White Crane Newsletter* (Summer 1990), p. 4.

19 *Ibid.*, p. 5. Robert Barzan is a former student of mine.

20 This does not mean that gay men must not utilize other ritual resources. Two books which could be helpful for them are the already mentioned Cherry and Sherwood, *Equal Rites*, as well as Elizabeth Stuart, *Daring to Speak Love's Name: A Gay and Lesbian Prayer Book* (London: Hamish Hamilton, 1992). Some books for personal reflection are: Amy E. Dean, *Proud to Be* (New York: Bantam, 1994) and Joseph Neisen, *Reclaiming Pride* (Deerfield, FL: Health Communications, 1994). An especially good book of reflections on Scripture for gays and lesbians is Chris Glaser, *The Word Is Out* (HarperSanFrancisco, 1994). I am indebted to Xavier Seubert for the additional following reference of an example of gay appropriation of religious ritual: John Nalley, 'Havdalah: a metaphor for queer lives', *Harvard Gay and Lesbian Review*, 3 (4) (1996), pp. 16–17.

21 Lesbians also can find resources in Women Church, a movement that has groups of Roman Catholic women gathering for worship without the presence of an ordained priest. Dream work can stimulate the imagination to assist in the invention of rituals. See Robert A. Johnson, *Inner Work: Using Dreams and Active Imagination for Personal Growth* (HarperSanFrancisco, 1986). For general background in doing dream work, consult Jeremy Taylor, *Dream Work: Techniques for Discovering the Creative Power in Dreams* (New York: Paulist Press, 1983). Robert Bosnak explores the places of dreaming among the Australian Aborigines in his *Tracks in the Wilderness of Dreaming* (Bantam Doubleday, 1996).

22 Cherry and Sherwood, *Equal Rites*, pp. xv–xvi.

23 Leech, *Soul Friend*, p. 89.

24 John J. McNeill, *Taking a Chance on God* (Boston: Beacon Press, 1988), p. 127.

25 Many younger people today embrace Christian values but have little to do with institutional religion. They are looking for a simple, evangelical presentation of Christianity. We can only hope that, as they mature, they will see that the spiritual life is not only a Jesus-and-me relationship, but that salvation comes through community. If we are to identify with the Catholic, Lutheran or Presbyterian communities, for example, it seems impossible to avoid the institutional church altogether. We have that strange expression 'I am a non-practising Catholic (Christian)'. It can be helpful to explore the meaning of such an expression with directees who use it, and this may open up many areas for examination. Surely, the statement means more than 'I believe, but do not practise my belief'. Belief without practice is no belief at all.

26 McNeill, *Taking a Chance on God*, p. 182.

27 Cleaver, *Know My Name*, p. 141. This theme is developed in terms of gay rights in secular society and the full acceptance of gays into the mainstream by Bruce Bawer in his popular book, *A Place at the Table* (New York: Simon and Schuster, 1994).

28 James L. Empereur SJ, *Models of Liturgical Theology* (Nottingham: Grove Books, 1987), p. 39.

29 *Ibid.*, pp. 40–1. For a telling story of how highlighting the prophetic quality of the liturgy can be threatening to a publisher closely associated with the Church of England, see the preface of Dr Elizabeth Stuart to her book, *Daring to Speak Love's Name: A Gay and Lesbian Prayer Book*.

30 In cases where the director is the one who touches, I am usually referring to the situation where the person who does body-work also does spiritual direction and vice versa.

31 By 'professional' I do not mean anyone who does massage or some other kind of body-work. There are an increasing number of professionals who take what they call a more 'spiritual' approach to this work. Directors should make referrals to those whose work has a more spiritual character, a more 'sacramental' dimension.

32 Some books the directees can use on their own would be: Dr John Schreiber, *Touching the Mountain: The Self-Breema Handbook, Ancient Exercises for the Modern World* (Oakland, CA: California Health Publications, 1989); Gay Hendricks and Kathlyn Hendricks, *At the Speed of Light: A New Approach to Personal Change through Body-Centered Therapy* (New York: Bantam, 1993); and Sophia Delza, *Tai-Chi Chuan* (State University of New York, 1985). The Feldenkrais method is

especially good for increasing our self-awareness. See Moshe Feldenkrais, *Awareness through Movement: Easy-to-Do Health Exercises to Improve your Posture, Vision, Imagination, and Personal Awareness* (HarperSanFrancisco, 1997). An excellent book for the beginner is *Awareness Heals: The Feldenkrais Method for Dynamic Health* by Steven Shafarman (Addison-Wesley Inc., 1997).

33   For the need for men to listen to their bodies, to nurture them and to experience them as a source of wisdom see Stephen B. Boyd, *The Men We Long to Be* (Cleveland: The Pilgrim Press, 1997), Chapter 7, 'On being body-selves: body and wisdom and body care'.

34   Body-work covers a whole range of experiences. I refer to a number of methods in this chapter. In general body-work refers to any form of treating the body by oneself or by another which is intended to enhance the experience of the body. For instance, there are many forms of massage. Some body-work seems indistinguishable from aerobics. Other kinds are very subtle and engage the imagination to a greater degree, such as chakra work. See Anodea Judith, *Wheels of Life: A User's Guide to the Chakra System* (St Paul: Llewellyn Publications, 1992).

7

Spiritual direction and the Conformist gay

These final three chapters are devoted to spiritual direction with the gay directee at different stages of adult development. Although I am often speaking to the director, the material here can be read by the directee with profit. This is especially true of the second and third stages of development where there is more possibility of mutual engagement in the process of direction as well as self-direction itself. Because we are not usually doing spiritual direction with children or even adolescents, we need to be aware that the directees as adults are not only each individually unique but also that they will be at some point in their growth as an adult human being. Adult development takes place in stages. We cannot naively presume that what is an issue at one stage of growth will be present at all levels. My presupposition is that people's spiritual growth normally follows their psychological growth. It may be that either kind of growth will be ahead or behind the other to a certain degree but it seems impossible to have a great disparity between the two.

Stages of growth are a common way of speaking about development in the psychological fields. These categories have been taken over by some of the writers on spiritual direction. I am following the work of one writer, Elizabeth Liebert, who has articulated three stages of adult development based on the larger body of work on the stages of growth. I am basing this discussion on the three stages described in her book, *Changing Life Patterns: Adult Development in Spiritual Direction.*[1] The three stages she has developed in detail are: Conformist, Conscientious and Interindividual. In themselves these labels are limited in their use.

More nuance is required and Liebert supplies that as she develops the main characteristics of each stage as well as the various transitions between the stages. A chapter will be devoted to each stage. I follow her content but will not use the more technical subtitles she employs.[2]

The Conformist stage[3]

It would not be unusual to have a directee begin direction firmly established in this first stage. On the other hand, this should not be presumed. Any individual directee may have advanced on their own because of their personal history. They may have been in direction before with someone else. We will have directees at any of the three stages or transition points. Nor can we presume to place one person totally in one stage without traces of the previous or hints of the next stage being evident. The Conformist stage is probably based on what is left over from our adolescence. The major characteristic of this stage is the importance of belonging. The reality of Conformist people is made by the groups to which they relate. All sorts of relationships can constitute their person-hood. It may be their family. It is often their peers. Sometimes their ethnic and cultural background is the determining factor and for the Christian it may often be the Church, doctrine or Scripture which tells them who they are. The point is that they conform in order to be able have an identity. They even conform to non-conformist activity.

People at the Conformist stage are not given to being very nuanced in their thinking and judgements. They tend to see things as either/or and in black and white terms. They can base their views of others on stereotypes and they do not easily make allowances for individual differences. And while they might not think that all people are alike, they do believe that all people of a certain kind are alike. They make judge-ments about others in terms of their reputation, what they have done, where they are on the social scale, and who they are in terms of career and money. They do not have a strong inner life. It has not yet been sufficiently developed and so they must rely on what they see on the outside for making any judgements about themselves and others. Because they do not know how to look inside themselves they have difficulty distinguishing among their feelings.[4]

The process of growth for the Conformist person is the gradual recognition of the inner movements of their interior life. This is a slow process because they do not know how to pay attention to the inner world. They are unable to describe their feelings except in a general way. The director can help them by having them revisit feelings from the past as well as the ones they are now experiencing. The director can supply for their lack of articulateness about feeling by suggesting feeling words. The point to this is that their feelings are important in their spiritual life and need to be admitted into their prayer life. Although not easy, it is possible to help them move from the externals of their life to the inner world and to assist them in finding a variety of feelings there.

Because Conformist people place such high value on group identity and group values, they find physical and social appearances to be very important. The same can be said for status symbols such as dressing styles, academic degrees, offices and cars. They tend to overrate these. When we work with Conformist people we must also concentrate on concrete behaviour and external norms. What we recommend for their spiritual growth will usually start with something tangible such as certain forms of prayer and reading. This can help them make distinctions in the area of the concrete between what is essential and what is not. From there we can encourage them to think for themselves. This is a complicated process because so much of their thinking had been done for them by family, friends or church. I would begin by letting them feel that they are free to search for God wherever God may be for them. They will need some help looking.

Since the observance of rules is a way of belonging to a group, rules are important to Conformists. For Christians this often means the laws of the Church or the precepts of the Bible such as the Ten Commandments. Because they are not very well acquainted with their inner lives, they cannot claim an inner authority. So, they rely on the approval of external authority, whether it be that of church, peers, or the expectations of the culture. One way the director can help break through this is by helping them to see the contradictions that will show up in their own rigid attachment to rules.

Because the Conformist's world is governed by a lot of shoulds, they are often very hard on themselves. They will want to deny any feelings that they consider to be negative such as their sexual attractions or their anger. They should be encouraged to look at any embarrassment or avoidance in connection with sexuality and anger because that may indicate that these are primary issues for them. Are they bringing with them an idealized sense of God which makes them uncomfortable with sexuality and anger? Do they have an exaggerated sense of sinfulness or are sexuality and anger viewed as something dirty or bad? Spiritual direction should bring these people to an acceptance that all feelings are good and loved by God. It is not unusual that shame will be part of the experience here and the director needs to be clear what is really sinful, and so shameful, and what need *not* be a source of shame. But as long as they are firmly at the Conformist stage this distinction may remain more on the cognitive level for them.

As already noted, the one thing we clearly experience with Conformist people is their desire to belong. They connect well with groups and they can find trust and warmth there. It may be the people with whom they work; it may be their bridge club; it may be a parish organization. There is a real connection although it is mostly on the conscious level because of their lack of awareness of unconscious motivation. Relationships are defined in terms of actions. For instance, they would define friends as people with whom they relax or spouses as people with whom they form a family. What deeper feelings and motives may be there are not accessible. Or when feelings are expressed they are done in a vague way.

Conformists who have a strong belief in God will relate to that God personally although the image of God may still be that of a strict parent and a demanding judge. They want to do God's will but someone has to tell them what it is. So they rely on the rules provided by a source outside themselves. They check in with some kind of authority. They take a somewhat fundamentalistic view of Scripture as they look for approval or the lack of it. All this comes from the fact that they have not yet freely chosen who they are and they have not yet clearly appropriated themselves. But they are also generous, helpful and consistent in furthering the goals of the groups to which they belong and in this the director may have that necessary opening to move them along in their spiritual journey. I now look at two main issues which director and gay Conformist directee will need to address: the need to belong and the undeveloped inner life. I conclude with a section on the passage into the interior life.

The need to belong

Since without relationships to groups Conformist people do not know who they are, they hold on tightly to them. Dissolving such relationships can feel like the disintegration of their personhood. Gays do this in the same way as heterosexuals, but there are some issues which are particular to them. The director will want to make sure that these are addressed and not left unsaid in the interaction with the directee. I focus on three areas: the need for a family, the experience of coming out, and the connection with the 'gay sub-culture'. At later stages of development some of these issues will be less pressing but at the Conformist level it is important to be explicit about them.

The need for a family

Directees may well begin direction with conflicts and feelings arising from their relationships with their biological families. When the family of a gay person knows his/her identity, there will be as many responses to this as persons involved. Rejection, acceptance, indifference, disgust, appreciation, envy, confusion, guilt, self-accusation, ignorance and anger are all some of the reactions that may meet the gays in their families. There may be a sense of loss of a son or a daughter and the need to grieve over that. Even when the family is accepting and place love of the children above all other considerations, refusing to treat them any differently than before, there still lingers in the background a certain 'wondering' about the fact that they are different. Many a mother has told me that if one of her sons turned out to be gay she would still accept and love him like the other children. But many also confess that they find it difficult to envision how two men can have the kind of relationship which would involve sexual expression.

Since for heterosexuals there is often a supportive family from which they come and to which they return, it is only natural that gay persons would desire the same experience. Probably most gays, and certainly those at the Conformist level, seek to create a 'family of choice'[5] in some way. They are driven to do so in the face of the clear homophobic messages some biological families send. Or they never come out to their families because they may be afraid that if they come out to family members the family dynamic will change with resulting pain and separation.[6] They need to find a parallel family. Even gays who come from families which are more accepting seek these families of choice. Siegel and Lowe comment that:

> In families where a gay member is completely and lovingly accepted, where his sexuality is no more an issue than his height or his hair

color, he still is alone among family members with his feelings about who he is and where he fits into the larger society. He has no one in his family of origin who feels quite the way he feels about life, who views the world quite the way he views it.[7]

The chosen family of each gay person is different. It can include friends and family members, people he or she has come to know in work, school, recreation and certain organizations. It will include both homosexuals and heterosexuals. It will be people with whom gays find a connection, those who bring meaning to their lives and to whom they can offer something back in the way of acceptance, compassionate listening, loyalty and healing. Siegel and Lowe say of this:

> As his healing continues through the acquisition of friends with a deeper empathy, the individual is admired, uplifted, invited to share in experiences that allow him to feel good about himself and admire characteristics in others that he finds reflective of his own. In the process of forming a family, he salves and, over time, heals injuries caused by past disparagements, and he discovers a sense of wholeness and harmony in his new surroundings.[8]

The director can only applaud the energy and creativity that a gay person puts into this process. However, at the Conformist level s/he would do well to have the directee examine this new family. The director could ask questions such as:

- Does she need it more than it needs her?
- Does he know who he is apart from this family?
- In what ways is she conforming to their expectations?
- How healthy is this new family?
- Has he replaced the possible dysfunctionality of his blood family with the dysfunctionality of another kind of family?
- What has she gained or lost by close identification with this family?
- Has he lost his own identity in seeing himself as part of these people?
- Has it increased her alienation from others, especially her blood family?
- To what degree has this pushed him to the margins of society even more?

- Has she lost a sense of balance between being someone who is different and someone who participates in the mainstream of life?

The director will want to pose these several questions during the period of time that the directee is mainly in the Conformist stage. At the same time it is important that the director affirm what is going on for the persons, namely, they are creating a way for themselves to be in the world, a world which is very homophobic, a place where they can recoup some of the loss of self-esteem as well as engage in the process of learning to think for themselves. Conformists need to be encouraged to look at their new relationships as a place where they can grow in a deeper understanding of themselves rather than a place which will only reinforce their tendency to see everything in clear categories, especially of that of gay versus straight. The danger at this level is that their identities will solidify at the Conformist level itself because they have let their need to belong dominate their lives.

The coming-out process

Another helpful area to explore in direction at this time is the coming-out process.[9] How did this happen for this directee? How much? How little? To and with whom? Each one's geography will be different. Siegel and Lowe say that gay men have established a new network of friends and connections as part of the coming-out process.

> In this stage of the coming-out process, his social identification with gay men helps to shift his self-concept from *homosexual*, the dominant society's name for who and what he is, to *gay man*, a new name, and a new defining category, with its own social rules and cultural knowledge.[10]

That may be true, but there are pitfalls here. This could lead the gay man to define himself over against others, by seeing himself in terms of what he is not. The director should not expect that gays at the Conformist level will have achieved much of a balance here. In fact, they may resist any relativizing of their identity which has been clearly drawn in terms of what straights are not.

Bruce Bawer rightly points out that recognizing one's homosexuality is different from sharing that with friends, families and co-workers. He says that the term 'coming out' has certain difficulties because it 'reduces a complex psychological and social process to a simple cut-and-dried one time ritual'.[11] There is no reason to believe that dealing with one's sexual orientation is best done by telling as many people as possible. Bawer notes that the words, 'closet', and 'being out', as used today, are terms which imply that those who choose not to reveal their homosexuality are less frank, less understanding of the self, and less self-assured. This ignores the many legitimate reasons that some gays have for remaining silent. Many of these reasons are based on differences that are cultural, familial, social and professional. This is an important reminder when dealing with gays who are considering coming out or in the process of doing so. Their involvement with the gay sub-culture may move them in the direction that coming out is the equivalent to being honest and that remaining in the closet is equal to deception. Coming out may release a lot of inner tension in an individual but it does not automatically produce a healthy person.

Although the coming-out experience is one frequently found at the Conformist level, this does not mean that all these gay persons, or even the majority of them, actually come out. That process may be delayed until the next level of growth because the Conformist's desire to belong requires him to stay in the closet. In the case of the directee who is not out the director will want to see how resolved this issue is. Does it reinforce a smothering or spirit-denying kind of belonging to certain groups which may have some homophobia in their ranks? For gay persons who are out the director would want to begin probing the various family issues. Often people are blind to the dysfunction in their own family until something shocks them into reality. The way their parents and siblings reacted to their homosexuality might serve as that shock. How have their relationships changed since coming out? What method did they use to come out and was it consistent with their personality? In other words, how forced was the experience for them and for others?

In many gay people at the Conformist level the director will experience in the directee an inner debate about whether they should come out or not, especially to their parents and family. I have often wondered why some gay people feel so much pressure, such an imperative, to tell their parents about their sexuality although they know that the parents are not psychologically able to deal with the issue. There is no way we can get people to accept us if they are not ready to do so. It seems to be more a matter of the gays' inability to accept themselves.

This is not to say that a person should not come out. But that should not include forcing it on others, demanding that they accept you as you are.[12] Others would argue that sometimes people need to be forced to look at their biases and coming out can do that.[13]

Thinking about coming out or actually coming out is a good time for directees to look at the relationships in their lives. Reflection on coming out to others can open up the kind of dependency they may have on these other people. It may reveal their own rigidity in their thinking that people should accept them. It may help them to see how caught they are in certain parts of the gay sub-culture with its political call for all gays to be out, and out in a certain way. This may bring them to a greater realization of how close they are with certain people, what the nature of their relationships is in reality, and what responsibilities they have toward them. The question is: are they still letting themselves be defined by their relationships to such a degree that they feel impelled to come out to certain people? These reflections are appropriate for gay people at the Conformist level. The other levels of development deal with coming out in different and far more positive ways.[14]

The gay sub-culture

Finally, it may be important for the director to discuss with the directees the degree to which they participate in what is called the gay sub-culture, especially its less positive aspects.[15] Especially at the Conformist level the meaning of going out to gay bars, going to gay dances, frequenting gay sections of cities, or enjoying homoerotic films needs examination. Director and directee need to know to what degree any of this activity furthers the growth of the directees and to what extent it keeps them at the Conformist level.[16] It is the responsibility of directors to keep themselves informed about the gay sub-culture so that they can assist their directees to find the healthy and positive aspects of this experience. Frank Browning in his *The Culture of Desire*[17] has done an analysis of the gay scene to explore the question: is there a gay culture? Is this culture created by gays themselves or by the straights who want to categorize the gays as a way of reinforcing their own identity?[18] I recommend the last chapter of his book, 'Paradox and perversity', to any director, not because it is a description of a sub-culture, but because of what it says about the gay experience, *queer* sensibility, in the context of contemporary understanding of what it means to be human. He says 'There lies the

essence of camp sensibility, of *queer* sensibility: an intimate acknowledgement that there is no centered, secure self, that the modern self is a
fluid fiction.'[19] This more post-modern view of the self permeates the
self-understanding of not only gay people but all in the larger culture.

Browning argues persuasively that if a gay culture exists it is because
it raises the critical issue of what kind of desire is acceptable and how it
can be expressed. The attitude of the military toward homosexuality is
the clearest example of what Browning means. Its concern is about an
'unrestrained desire that could lead to a breakdown of discipline and
authority'.[20] If the majority cannot suppress forbidden desire (between
two people of the same sex), then, at least, it can be allocated to a distinct
group of people called homosexuals. The issues that arise for Conformist
gays are: how do they feel about being categorized as people of unrestrained desire, how do they feel when their straight male friends may
wonder if they are becoming the object of their gay friend's affection,
how do they feel about being defined in terms of forbidden and unnatural
desires? Whether the feelings are negative or positive there is material
here for reflection.

A positive response to these questions carries with it the possibility
of gays locking themselves into a kind of cultural prison while a negative
response may reveal a whole network of relationships which lead to
self-depreciation. For Conformists who need to belong in order to know
who they are a close identification with the gay sub-culture could cause
considerable conflict. Although many feelings will emerge in this reflection, the feeling I would focus on is anger. At this level, it is anger which
holds the greatest possibilities for moving to the next level. The energy
surrounding anger is more accessible at the Conformist level than the
energy which accompanies sexuality. Conformist gay people may have so
identified with their sexual energy that it cannot be separated off from
the rest of their lives. This would preclude any serious reflection on it
on their part unless their anger introduces a middle ground between
themselves and their sexual energies.

An underdeveloped inner life

Much that characterizes the Conformist person is due to a weak interior
world, or more accurately, a fragile connection with the inner life. To
put it simply, they manifest a lack of depth. They make their human
connections on the conscious level since they do not have sufficient

access to the deeper self. This is the reason for their stress on the importance of externals in defining the self. To make deeper personal connections the person must pay attention to the inner movements of the soul. When we are unfamiliar with our interior geography we become uncomfortable with it as if we were wandering through an area where we had never been before. Often we are alienated from this inner world because each time we make a foray into it something emerges which threatens our peace. It is not only the unconscious part of our inner life but also that part which is accessible which demand recognition and which if they are denied will wreak havoc with a settled way of life. Whatever else Conformists are, they are certainly people who try to keep everything in order externally. This accounts for their dependent relationships and their black and white thinking. Even God is imaged in terms of an external relationship, the kind one might have with a strict parent.

For Conformist gay persons this lack of inner connection may mean that they are not very clear about their sexual orientation. They may be having sexual encounters with other men or women and still not be able to claim their gayness. Or being a gay person may mean no more to them than that their genital energy moves in a same-sex direction. Clearly, the director cannot start with these people by emphasizing the wholesomeness of the personhood of the gay person. They do not know who they are. It would hardly be possible for the gay man or woman at this level to have a healthy and sustained relationship with another man or woman, that is, one which moves them away from exploitation to growth. The goal of direction at this time is to move to self-appropriation, not only of their sexuality but of their entire self, outer and inner. The director had best begin with the concrete behaviour of the directee whether it is relational or not. The directees must come to some clarity about the meaning of their actions. They must begin to pay attention to what is happening inside of themselves when they act. They must be challenged to find an interior side to each of their exterior activities. The main purpose of the director here is to help gay people avoid vagueness about what is going on.

The Conformist person has no true inner authority. Because of that, Conformist gay persons are still subject to negative imaging coming from institutions such as the Church, cultural settings such as their families, and social contexts such as their jobs. These are false authorities which have been brought inside and are mistaken as the authorities of the

Conformist person. Lack of their own authority means lack of freedom. When such freedom is deficient there is little awareness of our spiritual possibilities. We respond to situations not from inner convictions but according to some rules, those of others or our own which we have interiorized. Or we reject and go against the rules of others. We see here the Conformist's lack of attention to the inner structure of the person. They have little to hold on to because the lifeline to the inner self is so tenuous. The director can help the Conformist directees by having them compare their authorities until they have some sense of those which come from their own convictions.

The Conformist gay or lesbian without inner power will probably be hard on themselves. Those of us who have done spiritual direction with gay people recognize this kind of directee. There is a great deal of self-depreciation, a kind of tossing and turning in the direction of life because they are taking their cues, all of them negative, from differing sources, both inner and outer. There is a sense of hopelessness or defeat because they feel they are predestined to act in a certain way sexually. And yet they receive no support for it. The message from the churches only confuses them more since these religious communities say they are good but what they do is bad. Because they have no inner authority to counteract the outer authority, the latter wins. And it is the latter which condemns them, alienates them and excludes them. And because they cannot find the God within there is nothing to balance the God from outside whom they perceive as condemning them also.

And finally Conformist persons have little access to their feelings. Here, feelings are not just external activities. To be in contact with feelings is to be in contact with a large part of our inner world. We must pay attention to feelings in order to connect with them. As I have noted the most important part of any spiritual direction, and certainly, in the beginning sessions, is the ability to distinguish thoughts from feelings. This is more difficult than we think. But unless we can do it, further growth is impossible. Growth takes place through clarification and as long as feelings are expressed in a vague way the passage to the inner world is inhibited. How could the director recommend the use of the affections in prayer if the directees do not even know what they are feeling? Feelings need to be named. One task of spiritual direction at this time is to become articulate about our feelings.

We find this lack of connection with feelings in the Conformist gay directees even in situations of intense emotion such as the death of a dear one from AIDS or the ending of what was hoped to be a permanent relationship. The director needs first of all to be emotionally supportive in such situations but s/he can also seize the opportunity to move the directees to name the various thoughts, feelings and bodily sensations that are present. They may not be very good at it but at least the more intense situations help them break through the defences they put up to avoid beginning that journey inward. Probably only at the highest level of adult development will gay persons be able to distinguish bodily resonance from emotionality, but the task can start here. At the Conformist level the director should not expect more than some ability to distinguish thought from feeling.

Starting the process of accessing feelings is immensely important at the Conformist level because so much of the feeling dimension of the person is being denied. This is especially true of anger and sexuality. At the Conformist level there is the possibility that both gay and straight persons can be sexually active, but out of contact with their sexuality. As a consultant once remarked to me when I was speaking with her about an acquaintance of mine who seemed to be very sexually retracted, 'When he wants to know what to do sexually he consults his head and not his genitals.' What she meant by that is that feelings were taking place in his body but they had been separated off from conscious experience so that the only thing conscious about them was what was going on in the head. My acquaintance was aware of being sexual or of the desire to be sexual, was conscious of his need to express himself sexually, but would not make his connection with another on the feeling level. It was an intellectual endeavour on his part. This intellectualization is not the equivalent to being reflective about sexual activity. Reflection, as opposed to mere consciousness, implies some perceptible level of integration. One can be conscious of what one is doing and be in denial about it at the same time. Denial provides the Conformist the opportunity to keep the feelings isolated from the rest of the person because in denial the feelings are immediately rationalized and, therefore, not directly experienced. Denial is understandable at this level since the person is not sure if there will be anything there when they explore their inner life. Dropping denial usually implies having achieved a level of trust of self.

On the other hand, some Conformists, including gay people, seem to think from their genitals, letting all decisions be made by them. 'Being led around by one's penis' is not the same as being in contact with one's sexuality. We are speaking here of the least developed of the Conformist gays and lesbians. These people do exist. We cannot presume that every one of our directees comes to us having already achieved considerable human development. Nor am I implying that the more mature one becomes the less there is of genital activity.[21] But as we shall see, the experience of being genitally active at the other levels is quite different. Perhaps, everything said thus far about the Conformist gay persons' weak inner world can be summed up by saying that they are not aware of their spiritual possibilities and making those available is what spiritual direction is about at this stage.

The interior passage

A helpful paradigm for spiritual direction is that of passage. Moving through the stages of adult development is a passage of maturing. The Whiteheads say: 'Journey, a metaphor of religious living, suggests the necessary mobility and peril, the discoveries and losses that pattern our Christian lives.'[22] The Whiteheads make use of the rites of passage studies of the Dutch anthropologist, Arnold Van Gennep, and the American anthropologist, Victor Turner, both of whom define passage in three stages: separation, marginality (liminality) and reintegration.[23] I suggest that the proper passage for the Conformist person is the Whitehead's first passage, 'an interior passage'. What I have noted above about Conformist gays and lesbians needing to belong as well as their undeveloped inner world needs to be seen in terms of what the Whiteheads say about the dynamics of passage.

> Psychologically, we grow by letting go of parts of ourselves no longer necessary for our journey; we are purified of parts of ourselves that do not fit the future. The reliance on parents, once so necessary, and the personal independence we develop in young adulthood must both eventually be let go of if we are to grow into the authority of our own adult lives and into mature intimacy.[24]

The Whiteheads speak of this passage as a movement toward self-intimacy. This acknowledging and embracing of who I am is what I have spoken of as self-appropriation. This is a passage inside and within myself with all my feelings, emotions and affections. 'Whatever decisions I will come to concerning the expression of my affection, I am invited in this first passage to befriend myself as *this* homosexual person created and loved by God.'[25] This is a terrifying passage for many gay people who have been socialized to keep themselves in the dark about who they truly are. It means letting go of the self-denial that may be an acquired part of their personality structure. Like every human being who moves inside, gay persons must wonder if they will survive this passage. What will happen if I admit to myself my real desires? But without this most foundational of all passages nothing further is possible. Any possibility of true love of self and of God is short-circuited. For gay persons there is no substitute for their love and acceptance of their true affective life. The Whiteheads observe: 'To deny the existence and goodness of my affections and of my affective orientation must necessarily twist my adult efforts of love and work, and thus must diminish my vocation.'[26]

Often this interior passage to religious maturity through self-awareness and self-intimacy is delayed. Conformist lesbians and gays may be in the midst of making it or may just be beginning it. Some seem not to have thought about it. This is the reason, as noted above, why there can be ambiguity about sexual orientation at this level. It could also mean that, as the Whiteheads point out, some gay persons have made some life decisions while still in the state of confusion which will need to be re-examined and this re-examination is resisted. Moreover, it will doubtless mean that all the sources of self-identification in them up to this point, such as participating in the gay sub-culture, will need to be scrutinized and often rejected. Directees cannot expect to have properly identified themselves in one spiritual direction session. This is a process which takes time. Not everyone who comes for spiritual direction and identifies himself as gay really is. Some are bisexual and some are heterosexual. Time and reflection will be needed to establish their identity. This is especially true if the directee is younger.

Many directors will find working with Conformist gay people a frustrating experience. Of all the stages of growth this is the one where there is the greatest resistance to growth itself. It is not immediately rewarding to work with people who have so little self-identity and who tend to live life so superficially, but as the Whiteheads remind us, this, like all transitions, is a sacred moment.

This time of self-examination and loss is also a period of opportunity and grace. Here, in the recognition of this passage as graceful, the Church's ministry to homosexual maturing begins. So frightened have we been of homosexual members of our mystical body that we have ignored the graces that have accompanied the quiet interior passage to self-acceptance of so many homosexual Christians.[27]

This movement out of the Conformist level is a rite of passage. But how can this be, if rites of passage are public events? This matter, especially in direction, is surrounded by confidentiality. The Whiteheads suggest that we can render this experience public yet protect privacy by sponsoring community discussions regarding homosexual maturing. Anything a director can do to create a more public atmosphere of acceptance through talks, writing or group discussions will help to lessen the marginality of gay Christians as they make their journey to God. It is also possible that the director and directee can ritualize their session occasionally. They might celebrate in some more formal or humorous way the movement to growth in the directee's life in some area. It is very easy to ritualize using some form of body-work. In fact, it is better to do bodily movement and touch in ritual form because that gives the people permission to do things they would be embarrassed to do outside of the session. Ritualized body-work is usually non-threatening. Some of this body-work may be just what the Conformist needs to move to the next step. When to use body-orientated rituals will be a matter of discernment. For some they might be ways of getting the directee motivated. For others it may be that they need considerable spiritual direction before they engage in any body exercises or prayer. The hope and intention is that as Conformist gay persons move to the next stage, they will have a stronger sense of personal identity, will be able to love more and work better. Loving and knowing themselves more, they are ready to move to the next step in their passage in the spiritual life.[28]

Notes

1 Elizabeth Liebert, *Changing Life Patterns: Adult Development in Spiritual Direction* (New York: Paulist Press, 1992).

2 In describing these three stages at the beginning of each chapter I am dependent on Liebert's analysis. The use of her ideas as well as her text will at times be close. To footnote every sentence seems both cumbersome and unnecessary. The word-for-word quotation of texts is, of course, footnoted. Her material is used with her permission.

3 These descriptions of the stages of growth may appear to the reader to be rather succinct and abstract. Hopefully, the application to the gay directee will flesh out these levels of adult development.

4   Distinguishing thought from feeling and among feelings themselves is, I believe, a
    necessary condition for growth in the interior life and for meaningful spiritual
    direction. Rik Isensee, *Growing up Gay in a Dysfunctional Family: A Guide for Gay
    Men Reclaiming Their Lives*, contains two chapters on feelings which are worth
    reading: Chapter 9: 'Working through feelings', and Chapter 10: 'Self-nurturing'.

5   Families of choice are described in Stanley Siegel and Ed Lowe, Jr., *Uncharted
    Lives: Understanding the Life Passages of Gay Men* (New York: Penguin
    Books/Dutton, 1994), p. 159. Also see Kath Weston, *Families We Choose: Lesbians,
    Gays, Kinship* (New York: Columbia University Press, 1991). The author deals with
    how we make families and develop kinship as gays and lesbians that is much
    stronger than biological connections. See Chapter 5 especially. See also Isensee,
    Growing up Gay, referred to above.

6   The National Conference of (US) Catholic Bishops' Committee on Marriage and
    Family Life has issued a statement entitled 'Always Our Children'. In it the bishops
    speak of the homosexual child as a gift. It appeals to parents to support their gay and
    lesbian children and to accept them without judging them. The bishops point out
    the problems that result when parents distance themselves from their gay children.
    While affirming the Church's position regarding the morality of homo-erotic acts,
    the document is very positive in calling for the acceptance of homosexuals in the
    community, for the recognition of the rights of gays, and that the attitudes of
    parents, priests and pastoral ministers 'follow the way of love'. I quote but one of the
    central statements of the document:

    > This child, who has always been God's gift to you, may now be the cause of
    > another gift: your family becoming more honest, respectful and supportive. Yes,
    > your life can be tested by this reality, but it can also grow stronger through your
    > struggle to respond lovingly . . . seek appropriate help for your child and
    > yourself. (See *National Catholic Reporter*, 10 October 1997)

7   Siegel and Lowe, *Uncharted Lives*, p. 160.
8   *Ibid.*, p. 158.
9   As the next chapter clearly indicates, coming out is also part of the Conscientious
    stage for many gays.
10 *Ibid.*, p. 158.
11 Bruce Bawer, *A Place at the Table*, p. 234.
12 For anyone considering coming out I recommend that they read the few excellent
    pages on it in Bawer, *A Place at the Table* (pp. 238–43). The director could profit
    from reading the whole book. Also, Tim McFeeley, 'Coming out as spiritual
    revelation', *Harvard Gay and Lesbian Review*, 3 (4) (Fall 1996), pp. 9–11.
13 That seems to be the presupposition of the two books of gay meditations, Joseph
    Neisen, *Reclaiming Pride* (Deerfield, FL: Health Communications, 1994) and Amy
    E. Dean, *Proud To Be* (New York: Bantam, 1994). There is also the phenomenon of
    'outing' others, that is, revealing the homosexuality of people who have not revealed
    it themselves. The champion of this outing is Michelangelo Signorile. It is not that
    Mr Signorile believes in indiscriminate outing, but he argues passionately that it is
    a necessary part of the gay agenda. See his *Queer in America: Sex, the Media, and the
    Closets of Power* (New York: Random House, 1993). He says: 'Journalistic outing is

not aimed at all gay people who are not following an "agenda", but at *public figures* and only when pertinent to a story that may or may not have anything to do with an "agenda" – liberal or conservative' (p. 149). Signorile says outing is not reporting on what people do in their bedrooms and that the purpose of outing is not to create role models. 'Outing may not be a vehicle to create living role models; it does, however, create visibility . . . Kids should know who's gay regardless of whether the people are proper role models . . . There's something to be said for *bad* role models. By exposing Malcolm Forbes we were trying to say to gay kids: Don't let this happen to you. Don't let your life be swallowed up by the closet though you're one of the richest, most powerful people in America' (p. 81). I do not find this book to be balanced. The author is clearly angry and labours under a similar presupposition to that of many African-Americans, namely, if one is black, then one must be actively involved in black issues. Signorile claims he is not invading anyone's privacy by outing them. But such outing still hurts. For a more balanced view see David Link, 'I am not queer' in Bruce Bawer (ed.), *Beyond Queer* (New York: The Free Press, 1996), pp. 266–78.

14 For directors who do not feel secure in their counselling or therapeutic skills I recommend that they read Chapter 7, 'Coming out', in A. Elfin Moses and Robert O. Hawkins, Jr., *Counselling Lesbian Women and Gay Men: A Life-Issues Approach* (Columbus: Merrill Publishing Company, 1982). In fact, I would recommend directors who have several gay directees to make themselves familiar with this book. There has been a great deal of writing regarding the coming-out process, much of it of varied quality. Some suggestions for further reading are: Chapter 3, 'Coming out to "blood" relatives', Weston, *Families We Choose*; Chapter 2, 'Breaking the bubble: care and coming out', Larry Kent Graham, *Discovering Images of God* (Louisville, KY: Westminster/John Knox Press, 1997). Leanne McCall Tigert, *Coming Out While Staying In* (Cleveland: United Church Press, 1996), is about her spiritual journey and sexuality. She speaks from a perspective of family-systems theory as applied to the Church and from a gay liberation-theology viewpoint.

15 It is also possible to speak of a gay culture which would refer more to the contributions of gay people to the arts, literature, music and the physical and human sciences.

16 For a balanced assessment of why many gays frequent gay bars see Bruce Bawer in *A Place at the Table*, pp. 252–3.

17 Frank Browning, *The Culture of Desire* (New York: Crown Publishers, 1993).

18 Browning deals with what I call gay sub-culture as well as gay culture. For a brief analysis of where the gay sub-culture has really reached the status of a true culture see Patricia Null Warren, 'A frontier culture', *Harvard Gay and Lesbian Review* (Summer 1997), p. 6. Daniel Harris, *The Rise and Fall of Gay Culture* (New York: Hyperion, 1997) laments gay men's loss of their radical position in society as they are being homogenized by the larger culture. He has been criticized for taking a too-simplistic view of mass culture and ignoring the influence of multiculturalism.

19 Browning, *The Culture of Desire*, p. 212.

20 *Ibid.*, p. 216. In *A Place at the Table* Bruce Bawer addresses the hostility towards the gays in the military in terms of the uncomfortableness of the heterosexuals. 'If many soldiers assume that their "right" not to be seen in the shower transcends the right

of the homosexual to serve in the military, so many civilians feel that their "right" not to have to be reminded that homosexuality exists outweighs the right of gays to live as openly as heterosexuals' (p. 120).

21 Nothing is implied by this statement about the morality of these actions. I am simply stressing that, perhaps more often than not, our directees will be dealing with genital activity, at least past genital expression, in spiritual direction. I find this to be true even in the case of a committed Christian who is following his/her church's teaching in this matter. The question particular to spiritual direction is 'what is the meaning of this activity in their movement towards God?' The responses of the directees will differ considerably, especially in the case of a directee who is unchurched, or does not identify with one of the Christian denominations, or whose faith commitment might be characterized as 'anonymous Christian'. In fact, my experience with heterosexuals is no different. Moreover, unlike the confessor, the spiritual director cannot deal with the directees here in a judgemental way. Their task is to assist the directees in discovering the meaning of this activity in their journey through wholeness to God. Often for the directees this will mean the conclusion of or regret about this activity. But in spiritual direction the directee must come to this conclusion. Whereas it may be appropriate for the confessor to refuse absolution in certain cases (of those Christians who go to confession), it would be totally inappropriate for the director to reject the directee in similar circumstances.

22 James D. and Evelyn Eaton Whitehead, 'Three passages of maturity,' in Robert Nugent (ed.), *A Challenge to Love: Gay and Lesbian Catholics in the Church* (New York: Crossroad, 1986), pp. 174–88. As will become clear, I find a connection between their three passages and the three stages of adult development of Liebert. There is further information about this first passage in McNeill's *Freedom, Glorious Freedom* (Boston: Beacon Press, 1995), pp. 64ff.

23 The work of these two anthropologists has been widely used by liturgical and ritual scholars for the past twenty or more years. I suspect most Christians became acquainted with these names through the work of liturgists. Someone interested in pursuing this matter further might well peruse Mary Collins OSB, *Worship: Renewal to Practice* (Washington, DC: The Pastoral Press, 1987).

24 Whitehead and Whitehead, 'Three passages to maturity', p. 176.

25 *Ibid.*, p. 178. This section is dependent on Whiteheads' chapter.

26 *Ibid.*

27 *Ibid.*, p. 180.

28 *Ibid.*, see p. 180 for this discussion.

8

Spiritual direction and the Conscientious gay

The transition to the Conscientious stage[1]

There is a transitional period from the Conformist stage to the next, the Conscientious. It is the nature of transitions that they are not easily recognizable. There are some tell-tale signs which may be summed up by saying that when the Conformist stage does not work any more, we are moving to the next. When the world can no longer simply be divided in black and white terms, when the communities to which we belong make contradictory demands, when the rules conflict, and when it becomes increasingly difficult to suppress certain human drives, we are in transit. The director's task is to help the directees not to turn around and go backward. Their experience is changing and they need support because this particular transition is not easy to make.

The movement to the Conscientious stage is one of growing self-awareness. Gradually we respond more to personal values than to group ones. The individual person is more important. We are more aware that rules are not absolute, more aware of ourselves in personal relationships, more aware of others as individuals, more aware of the need of personal autonomy. The coming stage is called Conscientious because more is now included in our consciousness. This expansion of consciousness means that we have increased our powers of introspection. We can now claim a personal vision. We take a greater interest in our relationships because there is more ability to explore them. This is a good place to be and for that reason it is dangerous. There may be the temptation to stay here. So many good people do. It may be that something external to us has to happen to propel us to continue our journey. Many people begin direction while in this transitional period. For gays it may be the death of a lover, a friend, or finding oneself to be HIV positive or some job rejection.

This is a movement into a period of liminality referred to in the previous chapter, that is, we experience ambiguity and questioning about so many things. This is the time of tossing overboard so much of the baggage we have accumulated as Conformists. Even God is not spared. Understandably, this time can feel empty and depressing. It will not help if the director does not allow the directee to experience this psychologically marginal time. Out of it can come a greater inner authority, more self-appropriation, and the power to reflect critically. We are now in touch with our inner life and we are discovering there a richness which will be the foundation for long term goals, realistic ideals and a sense of responsibility for our own life.

The Conscientious stage

As we move into this stage we see more of ourselves in context and community, more of our emotions, more of the patterns in our lives, more of how we interact in society. Because we see the consequences of our actions and the possibility of alternatives, this stage lacks the clarity of the previous one. We are more uncertain about who we are, what our purpose in life is, and what motivates us to do the things we do. This is the time of relativizing everything, including God. To make this passage alone asks a lot of us and thus there is a real need for spiritual companionship at this time. As the ground of faith shifts beneath our feet, we can experience a crisis of faith. Not only are we more in contact with our deepest beliefs but we also see them in comparison to other beliefs. Because we are more engaged with our interior lives we may experience many kinds of crises, whether it be rejecting our images of God as primitive and debilitating or rebelling against the structure of family and church. The purpose of direction at this point is to help the directee rebuild their identity. The accompaniment of the director is so necessary in this process because the directees are so vulnerable. They are now aware of the inner movements of their interior life but that does not mean that they can interpret them correctly. Here the director is called upon to bring in the skills of discernment to prevent the directee from making decisions based only on what they think is the right thing to do.

If at the Conformist level the emphasis was on the external, at the Conscientious it is on the internal, but it is the conscious rather than the unconscious internal which is our source of personal identity. To the extent that such a transition takes place we can say that at this level we know ourselves. We now operate out of internal standards rather than external rules. Our ideals and goals as well as our obligations are ours rather than those of a group or a relationship. The task in direction is not so much to make the directees aware but to help them deepen what they are now aware of. No longer caught up in the present moment the directees can take a longer view of themselves and so direction will take a different turn. The turn the directees themselves take now is more complicated. They are now aware of their motivations. They are finding that what was important to them in the past no longer is. Neither they nor God fit into things as in the past. I would describe this as a change from one symbol system to another, often spoken of today as a paradigmatic shift for the person. This may be a turbulent time but it is also the point when directees claim themselves as unique individuals.

Exploring the inner world

Since the movement is to the inner life, self-evaluation is now possible for the directees. Rules are self-chosen and internalized. Self-discernment is now possible. In fact, it is necessary. They understand the motivation behind their actions. They see more clearly their presuppositions and past assumptions. They are more willing to work with God rather than trying to save themselves. They also evaluate their present relationships. They can be more objective about them. Such clarity regarding their relationships makes it possible for them to broaden and deepen them. There is greater capacity for intimacy and there is more responsibility and communication in these relationships. Conscientious people learn from their relations because they hold them up like a mirror to see themselves more clearly.

As Conscientious people become more acquainted with their inner terrain, they are more able to differentiate among their feelings. Their ability to distinguish thought from feeling is enhanced. All this makes intimacy more possible. This contact with the inner life releases a great deal of energy that has been imprisoned. This means that they now have more to give to themselves and to others. During this stage they extend themselves to others to support and assist them. They do it from their inner authority and strength and not simply because the other person belongs to the same group as themselves. Conscientious people are people who care. But this usually means care for others and not for themselves. Self-care is something they still need to learn and spiritual direction will want to encourage them to move to self-care.

The more Conscientious persons care for themselves, the more they can care for others. And the more they care for others, the more they can deepen their relationship with God. God is now their God, not the God of their parents, their peers, their church, their groups, or their culture. God is now a personal God. The confluence of an experience of a more personal God and their being more in touch with their feelings will bring about a major change in the religious experiences of Conscientious level people. Prayer becomes more affective; God is imaged as friend or lover. They can express their feelings to God in a more comprehensive way. However, as open affectively as these people are becoming, they will still be reticent around sexual and aggressive feelings. They will be reluctant to get angry at God or to recognize fully their own sexual feelings. Obviously, at the least developed level people experience sexual feelings. This is usually done in terms of experiencing pleasure. What I am talking about at this stage is the ability to integrate these feelings so that when they feel sexually their whole body feels sexually. Conformists may not even know what that means. The more developed people become the more the sexual feelings are diffused from the genital area to spread throughout the person.

Although some directees will never reach this stage, most will. Spiritual direction is more truly spiritual direction at this level and also, usually more enjoyable. Directors are dealing with adults, people who are self-motivated, able to pursue long-term goals, and have some capacity to reflect on their lives. Naturally, this is not a problem-free stage of adult development. Being in greater touch with the self can also lead to a certain self-centredness. Having claimed their inner authority can also mean an excessive self-confidence in their own judgements and insights. Having now relativized their past world views, Conscientious people are often at a loss how to fit their newly claimed selves into the larger, ever changing, world. The director is here dealing with people who have integrity, are truthful, have high ideals, and understand the meaning of life. They are also aware of their responsibilities. This could mean that they will become cynical and alienating in order to avoid these responsibilities. The directors can help them not get side-tracked at this time. As they move the Conscientious directees to self-care, they will also help them extend their vision and their goals. This is the time to invite the directees to nurture their inner lives. I focus on two important areas for the Conscientious gay person in spiritual direction: a self-chosen identity and the passage to intimacy. I also briefly look at a tool so necessary at this stage: the discernment of spirits.

Self-chosen identity

For the gay man or lesbian who has successfully negotiated the movement through the Conformist stage to the Conscientious one, a great deal of deconstruction will have gone on. Much will have been and is being left behind. As the securities of the Conformist acquired through undifferentiated thinking and group identification disappear, the directee will experience loss.[2] Past life images have been lost and new ones must be created.[3] Gays in transition do not know which world they belong to. They have left many of their former ties behind and yet they cannot integrate into the heterosexual world completely. Their losses can be 'recast as essential birth pangs for the emergence of a more personally viable life image for gay men and lesbians'.[4] They have launched on a path of transformation. Several chapters in the book already referred to, *Coming Out Within*, detail the process of this transformation.

In a chapter, 'Initial awareness', the authors point out the difficulty of loss for gay men and women because the homophobia of society tends to exacerbate their losses. Gays may react even more strongly to these losses because of the structures of society which exclude them. Hopefully, during the Conformist stage the director could help these gays with their fears which explode when they are under threat. Still, loss at this level seems so great that they feel overwhelmed and may narrow their access to the feelings of fear brought about by some event such as testing HIV positive or the ending of a heterosexual marriage they may be in. The point is that their life image has been threatened and they react in fear.[5]

O'Neill and Ritter, the two authors of *Coming Out Within*, describe the kind of reactions that the fearful gay/lesbian person has. It is either holding on or letting go. The first reaction of holding on they describe by several examples of how this takes place. In summary they say:

The human organism can absorb only so much trauma at once without serious consequences and does its best to protect itself by throwing up filters that will gradually regulate the input of emotions and thoughts, allowing only a certain amount to be assimilated at once. In this process of regulating, people may feel as though they were losing their minds, behaving foolishly, or not acting like themselves: in fact they are probably doing exactly what they need to be doing to nurture themselves from becoming overwhelmed by grief . . . If one has a certain level of awareness of this, holding-on behaviors will probably be temporary. However, if these behaviors are relied on too heavily and unconsciously become a primary way of functioning in the world, a modus operandi, then the individual risks getting stuck at this point and may never address the true nature of his or her loss.[6]

This is the issue in a nutshell. The director's task is to assist the directee so that this is really a temporary situation. Much of what was quoted above about holding on may be the business of the Conformist stage, but very often much of this issue must be addressed when the directee is in the transiting stage, becoming more conscious. It can be helpful for director and directee to familiarize themselves with the many stories the authors relate in each chapter. They may find one or other story a 'close fit' to what they are dealing with at any particular time in direction.

The other negative reaction is letting go. This seems strange since ordinarily in the world of the spiritual life, letting go is seen as a positive movement to the next stage of spiritual growth. The letting go as a reaction to fear as described by the authors involves the acknowledgement of the losses by the denial of something in ourselves or our world. 'Letting go is a strategy of separating that which was once valued from the self.'[7] One of their stories communicates what the authors of *Coming Out Within* mean by letting go. It is the story of Connie who at an early age recognized her homosexuality. One night when sleeping in the same bed with her best friend, Glenda, she put her arms around her and tried to kiss her. Glenda reacted in fear and confusion and asked if Connie was homosexual. Connie denied it. But then she never touched anyone again. She became a recluse, living with her mother and hardly venturing out of the house. She denied part of her world, splitting it off from the rest of her. 'Central to her life image was to love and be loved by another human being. With this denied her, she let go of any further attempts to fulfill her dreams and escaped from life.'[8]

These two reactions are unhealthy. The only option for gay persons who continue to grow is to reconstruct themselves as they move into the Conscientious stage. Perhaps, the language of 'rebuilding' is not the most apt. It is more a question of claiming and reclaiming an identity already there. In an article, 'Claiming our identity as gift of God and love of Christ: reflections for spiritual directors', the author, a gay seminarian, puts the key question at this level of adult development this way: 'How do I claim an identity, not just in psychological terms but in faith as well?'[9] Finding one's identity has to be more than an the answer to an intellectual question. We can say that being gay is good and that we are happy that we are created a homosexual, but to be able to feel good about it is another matter. Feelings take time to catch up to insight. The insight into the goodness of being gay may come instantly in a moment of recognition when certain blocks have been removed. But the feelings will probably follow slowly behind. Nor will they come all at once. They may come in gradual steps, and usually there is no predictable pattern. The directee needs careful attention by the director as this is happening. The gay person's claiming of this identity on the feeling level may, in fact, often be facilitated by an intimate, genital relationship. Here the director needs to be especially sensitive, open and free of any presuppositions. Sexual experiences can as easily make the directee regress to the Conformist self-condemnatory stage as they can also become the opportunity to pursue the path to greater self-acceptance. It is quite possible that a directee who experiences fear of moving more deeply into self-intimacy will use sexual activity as a distraction from the deeper pursuit. Using sex as a way of avoiding intimacy is so prominent that it needs no proof. It is also possible that sexual activity for some directees will so help them to overcome their fear of the deeper pursuit that they can move more actively to embracing what is at times the more painful path of self-knowledge and growth. Each case is unique and the director needs to listen carefully to what is happening in the feeling world of the directee.[10] How gay people are evaluating these sexual experiences may well be irrelevant.[11] However, they should not prescind from these experiences as simply something passing. There is a great deal of information here and with the proper following and questioning the director and the directee can find ways to bring the gay person fully into the Conscientious stage. We must always keep in mind that even for healthy people on the spiritual journey it is always possible to regress to a previous stage, although for the growing person this will happen with less frequency.

The place of grieving in integration

Often full integration into this second level of adult spiritual growth will be preceded by some necessary grieving. John E. Fortunato, a gay therapist, has written a seminal book that many gays have found helpful, *Embracing the Exile*.[12] He claims that his work moves beyond traditional analytical psychology to include the spiritual dimension. What has impressed him in his work with gays is the fact that while they often enter therapy for the same reasons that heterosexuals do, their questions and concerns have a deeply spiritual aspect due to the severity of their rejection by society, family, and, I would include, church. The difference for gays according to him is that they cannot resolve their issues in the same way as heterosexuals. This is what he calls the gay predicament. 'For the gay person as well as the straight, the hope is for reintegration. But here the similarity ceases. Gays are blocked from reintegration within the mythic system. They are stuck with their frustrations. That's the gay predicament.'[13]

What Fortunato says about therapy is even truer of spiritual direction with the gay person. In order to negotiate through life where there is so much homophobia the directee must take on a perspective much larger than the myths by which society lives, 'a spirituality much more profound'. Both therapy and direction must awaken 'in the patient levels of consciousness far beyond those necessary for most straight people'.[14] As the title of book indicates, being gay is being in exile. It is the exile of the oppressed minority in union with other minorities. It is the exile of marginalization described in a previous chapter. It is the exile of growing up and living in a world where the norm is heterosexual. It is the exile in a culture whose paradigm of humankind is found in 'straight' role models and heroes.[15] It is the exile of worshipping in a Church whose sacrament of graced humanity is the marriage of a man and woman. This exile must be embraced and used as a way of deepening the spiritual life. It is here that the grieving process becomes necessary. Fortunato gives a litany of the causes of pain in the life of gays and lesbians. The spiritual director will recognize these instantly: loss of family connections, possible loss of job, being the subject of jokes and insults, etc. Grieving means letting go of the pain, letting this pain become your teacher to a deeper life.[16] Such grieving should be encouraged during the Conscientious stage. We cannot expect gay directees to let go of past securities and desires any more dispassionately than we would straight directees.

Gaining perspective

The combination of growing insight and grieving usually bring to gay men and women an ever-deepening feeling of healing. More peace is experienced. They are turning the corner on a negative past. Less energy is required to deal with the pain. Because they no longer avoid their fixations, but rather are going through them, they are finding that there is a positive side to what before seemed pure negativity. What is taking place is what the authors of *Coming Out Within* call gaining perspective. I cannot improve on their summary of this transition.

> A major reaction at this phase is the overall reduction of emotional intensity, characterized by patience and the tendency to release more readily hostility, anger, and resentments . . . Accompanying this softening of feeling comes a diminished need to struggle at reversing the loss or to continue doing battle with fate . . . As perceptions become more balanced, people often are more willing to forgive and accept themselves, others, or the incomprehensible powers that seem to direct their lives . . . When setbacks occur, balance, peace, and perspective have a greater chance of being regained.[17]

Moving through the stages of adult development with the transitions can be a perilous matter. The danger is that the directees can stop at any point and not move on. As they approach the more advanced stages of growth this is an increasing temptation because it is easier to feel comfortable with the degree of health already acquired. This is where some forms of therapy differ from spiritual direction in that the director must remain a gadfly of sorts, ever encouraging the directee to continue the journey. This voyage is an essential part of the creation of the self-identity of the gay person. Integration must take place at each of the stages of development, but the kind of integration called for at each level differs. At the Conscientious level integration of the gay's pain and loss means putting into action what the directee has become aware of. Insight into their situation in life leads to doing something about it. Past dreams have had to be left aside. New dreams of what they want their life to be like must be allowed to emerge.

But these dreams must be acted upon. To claim their self-identity gays need to ritualize their movement publicly.[18] For some it will mean that they come out at this time, or come out to more people, or come out in particularly difficult situations. I am not suggesting that Conscientious gays are to become militant activists, but this public ritualizing could be something like volunteering to work with people with AIDS. It could mean counselling other homosexuals. It could simply be a willingness to have open conversations with people about the meaning of being gay in the world today. It may mean forgiving people who have injured you because you are gay. Self-identity cannot remain purely interior. It must also have a public character.[19]

Reframing the gay reality

The final step of claiming self-identity at the Conscientious level is the reframing of personal reality. New self-images emerge as people move through their pain and loss and come out at the other side. Now gay persons have added energy to negotiate through life despite the pitfalls of homophobia that surround them. But more than that, this additional energy can be put to more creative uses. Life is more open-ended and far less predictable than at the Conformist stage. They are now really creating themselves, building upon the goodness of their lives that they have been uncovering as they moved into the Conscientious level. For Christians now much of the religious language of rebirth and resurrection takes on new and more concrete meaning. There is a feeling of being alive because they feel connected with so much more in the universe. Their enlarged world includes so many more people and events. The past is less of a prison and the future is less frightening. The conscious image of the self now reflects more closely the image of the deep self which is for the most part unconscious.

These gay men and women now have the personal freedom which allows them to move toward the unlimited possibilities of spiritual growth. They are ready to move on to the third stage of adult development, the Interindividual stage. The director will find that when gays reach this point in the Conscientious stage meditation through centring prayer will have great power and attraction. Christ himself as the object of prayer and source of identity will not only be the historical Jesus but also the embodiment of the wisdom image of the Old Testament, a Christ who is not genderless, but inclusive of male and female images. The figure of Wisdom in the Hebrew Scriptures is

> personal, female, and cosmic, having a functional equivalence with the activity of Yahweh in the self-understanding of Israel . . . For Paul, Jesus is the Wisdom of God and this identification of Jesus with the Wisdom of God links Jesus with the cosmic role of Wisdom in the Hebrew scriptures which is one of creating, caring and ordering the world and the affairs of history.[20]

Jesus is the male figure of the Gospels, but is much more than that. As Wisdom he includes in himself equally the feminine and the cosmic aspects of creation. This fully inclusive Jesus is the one to whom the Interindividual person can relate. At the Conscientious level gay persons can move away from the restrictiveness of the solely male Jesus. This is a freeing Christological experience for them and is one of the elements of their journeys through the Conscientious stage which should bring them the psychological and theological freedom necessary to move into the Interindividual world.[21]

The discernment of spirits

Leaving the Conscientious stage and moving into the Interindividual stage requires considerable discernment. It would be impossible to say where in the life-process discernment is more or less demanded. But both director and directee cannot afford to ignore the need for it. John J. McNeill has written about the power of discernment in his own life.[22] Following Ignatius of Loyola's understanding of discernment McNeill defines it thus:

> To *discern spirits* is to listen to our own hearts. Our God dwells within us and the only way to become one with our God is to become one with our authentic self. If any action we undertake brings with it deepening of peace, joy, and fulfillment, then we can be sure what we are doing is right for us. To be able to discern spirits we must have made a total commitment of ourselves to God and be willing to do whatever God asks of us.[23]

McNeill makes a very important observation, one to be noted in spiritual direction. He says that many gay people do not trust their feelings, especially feelings of affection and attraction. They try to live in their heads. They try to control their emotional life by over-valuing reason. But to do so is to miss the voice of God which comes to us when we trust our feelings and are open to experiencing our sexuality. In that sense discernment is more a matter of the heart than of the head. He gives the example of one of his clients who only permitted himself sexual experiences when intoxicated. But then this client began to develop a relationship and in the sexual exchange which followed he experienced deep joy, peace and fulfilment. But the homophobic tapes put in his head by family, culture, and church were still playing. He was tempted to cut off this relationship, stay in the closet, and go back to experiencing sex when drunk. That way he could blame alcohol rather than his fear of relationships.[24]

This fear of relationships is connected with a fear of God because of the person's image of God. It is still more one of fear than of love. At times it can be difficult for those at the Conscientious level to make the obvious connection that if God is a God of love, then it follows that they show their belief in that love by permitting themselves to love and to be loved. And that love and being loved for most people includes sexual expression. Whenever people say they love God and neighbour as them-selves in all ways, except one, the genital one, a warning signal should sound. God did not create us to be alone, to be without genital love. Obviously, genital love is not possible for all, due to circumstances, voca-tion, or the need to integrate certain gospel values in their lives such as celibacy, especially the celibacy that some churches ask of their gay members. The point is that all people look for love if they are honest with themselves. So many people never find that love. I find it especially touching in direction to have a directee who would and could really love another but the other never enters his/her life or does not respond with equal affection. There are also those who are loved by someone but are unable to return this love. Working with them will often be assisting them to look at the love that God has sent into their lives and to embrace it as a gift, a gift for which so many others long. Often honest sexual love, because it is so concrete, is the most human way of knowing if the love of God is equally concrete.

Discernment of spirits at the Conscientious stage is of particular importance because of what Ignatius calls the 'movements of the soul'. It is at this level of adult development that we are looking more deeply at our interior life. The way to attend to the inner world is by observing these movements of love, desire, hate, hope, fear, depression, bitterness, sweetness, etc. and any other interior movements which help or hinder us in our Christian lives. Spiritual direction at this stage will be very much about the various directions of our thoughts, feelings and bodily sensations we find present and to relate these to the more difficult to describe inner experiences we are having. We need to remember that these inner movements are the ordinary ones we all have.

> It would be a serious mistake to think that, in these rules, (*of discernment*) Ignatius is principally concerned with unusual, even sensational, spiritual experiences. The rules do help in dealing with these experiences, but what Ignatius is mainly concerned about is to help us understand and respond wisely to the ordinary spiritual or anti-spiritual movements of everyday Christian life.[25]

There is a threefold purpose to these rules. One, to get in touch with these various movements in us by being able to discriminate among them and to be able to reflect on them. Two, to see what influence these movements have in the way that we lead our Christian life, either positively or negatively, and to identify what spirits are influencing us. This is discernment properly speaking. Third, to allow ourselves to follow the good spirits, the Holy Spirit in Christian terms, and to avoid being caught by evil spirits, destructive forces in our world.[26]

Such discernment is so important for Conscientious gays since they more than straights will be experiencing conflicting interests and values. They will be called upon to make choices about their lives where often straights can depend upon the Church, family and culture to support their decisions. The gay man and woman will find themselves alone here. Thus, the need for a discerning spiritual director. Although Lonsdale is not addressing the situation of the gay person as such, he makes a significant point that applies to gays, and, in particular, in direction.

> In the discernment of spirits it is the deeper levels of affectivity that we are concerned with: those which actually influence our behavior; the areas where our affective life and the life of the spirit inter-penetrate; the places from which spring our commitments, our most significant choices and the fundamental directions that we give to

our lives. Discernment is mainly about these more significant areas of our affective life.[27]

Conscientious homosexuals can hopefully tap into that affective depth when dealing with issues of coming out, being more political, leaving a relationship, entering a relationship, being sexual. Lonsdale points out that it is not so important to know where the feelings are coming from or what they are in particular: joy, anger, guilt, etc., but rather the direction in which the feelings are leading. Working closely with the director gay directees can discover the spiritual values which are involved in following the direction of these feelings.[28]

A passage of intimacy

Both the transition into the Conscientious stage as well as the Conscientious stage itself can be called, in the Whiteheads' terms, a passage of intimacy. Having moved into their interior worlds, gay men and lesbians will find that they are challenged to move further. Having achieved a greater love of themselves, especially as gay persons, they are invited to enter another passage, this time with others. If the first passage is about self-acceptance, this second one fulfils 'the need and desire to be known and loved for who I am'.[29] This means coming out in some sense. I think coming out is an issue for gays at both the Conformist and Conscientious levels.

Many directors will find that they will dissuade Conformist gays from coming out because they have insufficiently developed their inner strengths. If they are still operating out of destructive anger or self-depreciation, they may make serious mistakes by coming out to people who are not ready or sympathetic. At the Conscientious level the director can be more confident that the directee will make the right choice in terms of those with whom they wish to share their homosexuality. Because at this level the directees have a greater awareness of the differences in their feelings and more insight into their internal geography, they may actually experience more conflict about coming out. They are clear that they want to share that part of their lives. But there is a risk involved. Some will receive their revelation in a supportive fashion but others will, if not reject them, at least feel and act differently toward them. The timing for coming out is an individual affair. Some come out to some close friends and co-workers and no one else. Some come out only to the spiritual director. Some are out only to their lover. Some come out to a variety of people who do not know each other and so a certain anonymity is maintained. Some come out to no one explicitly, but all their friends know they are gay. It is implicit in everything they do. Each of these ways has its own variation. The director needs to be sensitive to all these possibilities and not try to impose a way of coming out for his/her directees.[30]

Coming out to someone you love is an act of love, as is receiving the coming out of someone you love an act of love.[31] The Whiteheads make the point that the passage to the interior life (which I place in the Conformist stage) and the passage to intimacy go together. McNeill takes up this same point and offers some illustrations of it. Sometimes these two passages seem to be contemporaneous although the challenges differ. But usually the challenge to enter into the world of self-acceptance will be stronger for the Conformist person since that kind of work is a presupposition to moving into the second stage of adult development. The exploration of the interior life will continue at the Conscientious level but now it is done in conjunction with others. The Whiteheads make an observation on the interrelationship of these two passages which I consider excellent advice for the director of gays.

> We learn about our loveliness, whatever our sexual inclinations, by being loved. It is most often others who first announce to us the surprising news of our goodness and attractiveness. Yet our adult ability to love well – that is, to share our lives and bodies in honest and nonmanipulative ways – rests on an enduring confidence in our own loveliness. Convincing myself that God loves me when I do not love myself is a most difficult task. The lessons of my loveliness, learned from others and from God, must take root in me as a dependable conviction: this is the meaning of virtue.[32]

Many of us have had the experience of loving someone deeply when the other person cannot return our love. Most of the time it is that they cannot be open to receive love because they do not love themselves sufficiently. They say they know and feel they are loved by God. But I wonder how true that is. Perhaps, they know intellectually that God loves them. But how can they receive the love of God when they cannot receive the love of one of God's creatures? I can hear them say: 'But I do receive the love of others.' But is this any more than an intellectual recognition?

Do they respond to love with their hearts, and more importantly, with their bodies? This is one of those times when a person's incarnational theology is tested in the fire of ordinary human experience. This is an important point when directing the Conscientious gay person because it is at this level that intellectualization can substitute for experience. At the previous Conformist level directees often engage in a lot of experience (perhaps, including sexual encounters) with little or no consideration. When they move to the Conscientious stage it is important that they do not leave experience behind. Rather, now their experiences are situated in a context of theological and spiritual reflection. We should be more embodied, not less, as we move through the stages of development. Such embodiment, which presupposes a closeness to ourselves, will ensure that we do not move too quickly into the second passage of intimacy, skipping the first passage into the inner life. All must experience and affirm their own embodiment before they can experience and affirm the embodiment of another. There is no such thing as instant intimacy.[33]

Nor is there any intimacy without risk. The risk is in becoming close to someone. Hopefully, Conscientious gays will be sufficiently strong, having learned to love being gay, that they can invite others into their lives with an increasing degree of closeness. If they are healthy, they will invite both men and women. Intimacy does not have to imply genital expression. The Whiteheads remark: 'Decisions about sexual and genital expressions of intimacy are separable from this movement of intimacy; whether Christian adults choose a celibate or sexually active life-style, they must face this passage.'[34] We have no choice but to move into intimacy. To avoid this passage means that one cannot grow as a human being, cannot, in fact, reach or maintain the Conscientious level. And most significantly we cannot love God, except abstractly. A gay man or woman can only love others as a gay man or woman. Their love for God must be homosexual. Nothing else will work.

That is why spiritual direction is so important at this time. It is also the reason why it is very helpful for gay directees to find some support groups, gay organizations where they can find some home. Besides the director they need members of a group to help them make this passage. The first passage into the inner life can be fearful because this inner world is unknown. The second passage can paralyse gay people because of the self-exposure and risk when they offer their love to another and discover how vulnerable they are. In our culture people have sex indiscriminately and at a very early age. But there is little self-offering in such experiences. If anything, they disguise the true feelings and identity of the people involved. It often does not reach the level of human sharing. We say an integrated person is one who gives all of him/herself whenever they make human contact. When we offer our selves in an integrated way, we give the other all of our being. It is not that we lose our personhood in the other; rather we claim ourselves more deeply in such union. Spiritual direction with gays needs to give them a supportive environment in which to make possible their taking these necessary risks to grow in their relationship with God. At this point in direction the director might wish to suggest to the directees that they take part in retreats for homosexuals and that they participate in liturgies which are sensitive to gay persons and issues. Gays need these external supports so they can continue their inner work at this time.[35]

As directees move through this Conscientious stage, and especially as they come to the end of it and begin their transition into the next stage, they will be more and more painfully aware of how the Christian community has not been supportive of them. As the Whiteheads point out, that community which should be teaching them about the paschal passage of Christ, of the passage from death to life, from loss to gain, and from crisis to grace, has, in fact, required them to deny their very selves by denying them the possibility of maturing as a gay person. Rather they have had to seek maturity, first in anonymity, and then, in carefully guarded situations such as spiritual direction.

> With such a denial, the believing community forfeits its role of protecting and predicting this pattern of religious growth. Thus has homosexual Christian maturity remained closeted, hidden. Thus 'darkened', it could not perform its generative function: to witness to the next generation the shape, both its perils and its grace, of this Christian journey.[36]

McNeill, in elaborating on the Whiteheads, quotes from an article by Tom Clarke SJ, that 'to be deprived of one's story is the most ruthless form of oppression'.[37] This realization is a strain of deep sadness both for director and directee in a journey that has moved into the inner world and successfully made the passage into intimacy. The spiritual life of gay directees is now well developed. They know who they are and they have accepted and appropriated that identity. Their communion with God is secure. Their progress both on the interior plane as well as that of their personal relationships is evident. They are healthy gay people. And yet, there is this pain.[38]

Notes

1 This material dealing with the transition and the Conscientious stage itself is dependent on Elizabeth Liebert SNJM, *Changing Life Patterns: Adult Development in Spiritual Direction* (New York: Paulist Press, 1992), Chapter VI. It is used with permission.

2 When gays realize that they are not straight and cannot live that life, the losses could include family connections, acceptance by the Church, dreams of family life, and advancement in certain types of employment.

3 Craig O'Neill and Katherine Ritter in their book, *Coming Out Within* (HarperSanFrancisco, 1992), deal with this issue of loss in particular. Their chapter, 'Life image', details what this phrase means and how gays need to form new life images. I believe that any one who works with gays and lesbians should have this book ready at hand. It deals closely with many of the topics covered in this book. The subtitle is *Stages of Spiritual Awakening for Lesbians and Gay Men*. As with so much writing at this time in the area of gay spirituality, it has a strong psychological emphasis. It seems that spirituality detached from the Church or specific religious traditions has no vocabulary apart from the psychological.

4 *Ibid.*, p. 48.

5 See chapter on 'Initial awareness' for descriptive and fascinating examples of this withdrawal based on fear.

6 *Ibid.*, p. 80.

7 *Ibid.*, p. 95.

8 *Ibid.*, p. 100.

9 'Quiet pools and new strength: the spiritual direction of lesbian and gay religious and clergy', *CMI Journal*, **16** (Winter 1993), pp. 44–8.

10 As already noted, sexual activity on the part of the directee will often not arise in the dialogue between director and directee. When it does it may be referring to past activity only. Reflection on such activity can be a source of greater insight and growth for the directee. It may also be that the directee is at present sexually active. This too can be material for reflection and the director can help directees see how this does or does not fit into their spiritual journey in terms of their particular religious commitment and the religious tradition to which they belong. My point is that the director must follow the directees in these experiences to help them discover how God is moving them. It is pointless for the director simply to tell the directees that their conduct is wrong and that is the end of it. They can then simply leave the director's office and not return, and an opportunity to assist these persons will have been lost.

11 It is true that in themselves the actions may not be morally irrelevant. The point is that a moral evaluation of sexual activity is not enough to discover its meaning or how it might be integrated into one's journey, even if that means a form of celibacy. After all, for the parties in a heterosexual marriage to discover the meaning of their

sexual exchange much more must be done than simply to judge that it is morally acceptable.

12   John E. Fortunato, *Embracing the Exile* (HarperSanFrancisco, 1982).

13   *Ibid.*, p. 36–7.

14   *Ibid.*, p. 40. I agree in general with the author's analysis. But it also seems to me that this book, published in 1982, is now showing signs of being dated, especially in its rather black-and-white presentation of the pertinent issues. It is true that gays must go through a process of transcending society's view of them, of having a God larger than the culture, of discovering their own special place in the history of salvation, but that is true of heterosexuals as well.

15   There are an increasing number of homosexuals in the public arena who now speak of their gayness openly in the hope that it will create a different public atmosphere and provide some role models for gays.

16   Fortunato has been influenced by the psychologist, Sheldon Kopp. And so he moves away from an ego-orientated psychology to one more Buddhist in character. But Christians can easily find in his approach the elements of detachment as understood in their tradition. As a friend of mine put it: 'When the student is ready, the teacher will come.'

17   O'Neill and Ritter, *Coming Out Within*, p. 142.

18   For specific ways to do this see Kittredge Cherry and Zalmon Sherwood (eds.), *Equal Rites; Lesbian and Gay Worship, Ceremonies and Celebrations* (Louisville, KY: Westminister/John Knox Press, 1995).

19   See the chapter on 'Integrating loss', in O'Neill and Ritter, *Coming Out Within*.

20   See Dermot A. Lane, *Christ at the Centre* (New York: Paulist Press, 1991), for an elaboration of these points.

21   See the chapter, 'Reformulating loss', in O'Neill and Ritter, *Coming Out Within*. The subtitles of this chapter hint at the kinds of reformulation possible here: working through shame, being freed from jail, seeing life through a new lens, reframing assumptions, exploring new connections, flowing with life. These are the tasks which are taken on in an incipient form in the Conformist stage, become more intentional in the transitional stage and become a regular part of the person in the Conscientious stage.

22   In Chapter 5 of *Freedom, Glorious Freedom* (Boston: Beacon Press, 1995).

23   *Ibid.*, pp. 20–1. McNeill gives the impression that in the discernment of spirits God speaks directly to the person, bypassing the mediation of church, family and culture. As it stands such a comment is not wrong, but it does not say enough. McNeill is surely correct in saying that the messages from church, family and culture are polluted by homophobia. It is clear to me that God can bypass church and family in speaking to any individual. That God who became incarnate bypasses our culture when communicating with us would be more difficult to maintain. The issue is not really about mediation, but about the directee having qualified assistance during the discernment process. Such is the task of the director. Those of us who work in this area of direction know how easily the phrase 'discern God's will for me' is invoked to justify what we have already decided to do. It is also telling that so many who talk about discerning frequently leave out the 'of spirits' part. Unfortunately, today discernment has been trivialized.

24 *Ibid.*, pp. 23–4. In the dynamic just described, I find little difference between gays and straights. Being uncomfortable with sexuality and looking for a way to avoid dealing directly with it seems to come with being a member of the human race.

25 Jules Toner SJ, 'Discernment in the spiritual exercises', in John E. Dister SJ (ed.), *A New Introduction to the Spiritual Exercises of St. Ignatius* (Collegeville, MN: The Liturgical Press, 1993), pp. 63–72. I also highly recommend the chapter on discernment in David Lonsdale SJ, *Eyes to See, Ears to Hear: An Introduction to Ignatian Spirituality* (Chicago: Loyola University Press, 1990). Lonsdale defines discernment this way: 'searching honestly for the most authentic truth; not just the knowledge that can be learned but makes little difference to how we live, but all the deeper gospel truth that makes little sense in fact until it becomes the truth that governs our lives' (p. 63).

26 Lonsdale, *Eyes to See*, p. 66–7. Lonsdale is aware that the language of spirits may cause some difficulties for some. He notes that Ignatius was pre-Freudian and accepted the presupposition about the presence of good and bad spirits in human life. But that does not vitiate what he had to say about discernment. We are still searching for proper language here.

27 *Ibid.*, p. 70.

28 *Ibid.*, p. 72.

29 James D. and Evelyn Eaton Whitehead, 'Three passages to maturity', in Robert Nugent (ed.), *A Challenge to Love: Gay and Lesbian Catholics in the Church* (New York: Crossroad, 1986), p. 180.

30 Chapter 7 of McNeill's *Freedom, Glorious Freedom* gives some practical advice on coming out. The self-destructive behaviour that he refers to, such as coming out to homophobic parents in order to hurt them, is more likely to occur at the Conformist level. Part of the discernment called for at the Conscientious level is precisely to choose those who will respond to a gay person's coming out in a respectful and compassionate way.

31 See James D. and Evelyn Eaton Whitehead.

32 *Ibid.*, p. 181.

33 See the wise comments of the Whiteheads, 'Three passages to maturity' (pp. 181–2) and of McNeill, *Freedom, Glorious Freedom* (pp. 75ff.).

34 'Three passages to maturity', p. 182.

35 Again, I recommend what the Whiteheads have to say regarding moving into this second passage in terms of rites of passage. Their point is seconded by McNeill. By rites of passage they mean, besides spiritual direction and retreats, joining such groups as Dignity, Integrity, support groups, reflection groups, therapy and the like. Courage is a Roman Catholic group of gays and lesbians who promise to live out their homosexuality in a celibate life-style. McNeill takes a dim view of this group, calling it a binding together of gay members in self-hatred. Perhaps, but we must remember that there are gays as well as straight people who choose celibacy without taking a public vow of chastity. We should not presume that God does not issue such a call or that these people do not need support groups also. Self-destructive behaviour may go on in these gatherings but that is true with any organized group of human beings. However, it needs to be noted that some serious scholars of gay spirituality would not recommend Courage to those who have

chosen celibacy in a healthy way because the organization is seen as a way to keep gay men within the control and authority of the Roman Catholic position that all gay men must be celibate and that it has little positive notion of the gay life.

36 'Three passages to maturity', p. 183.

37 McNeill, *Freedom, Glorious Freedom*, p. 79.

38 At the present time the churches are struggling to find ways to mitigate any of the harshness of their past and present positions regarding the morality of homosexual acts as well as the place of gays in the church communities. The statement approved by the US Catholic bishops, 'Always Our Children: A Pastoral Message to Parents of Homosexual Children and Suggestions for Pastoral Ministries', is evidence of a church's desire to be more compassionate and understanding. Tension remains because homoerotic acts are still considered sinful by many churches. Spokespeople for the churches as well as theologians strain to emphasize the positive side of a church's position. An example of this would be Stephen J. Rossetti and Gerald D. Coleman, 'Psychology and the Church's teaching on homosexuality', *America* (1 November 1997), pp. 6–232. We are all indebted to such authors who place the most compassionate and pastorally sensitive interpretation on church statements regarding homosexuality. But for many of us, the need to protest so loudly the non-condemnatory and non-discriminatory nature of these pronouncements leaves us wondering to what degree they are really authentic expressions of Christ-filled communities. Some additions were made to the statement 'Always Our Children' to satisfy its critics. They do not change the message of the document (cf. *National Catholic Reporter*, 17 July 1998, p. 12). Also, it is important for Roman Catholics to note that although the 1975 *Declaration on Sexual Ethics* claimed that the inclination itself is disordered (n. 8), the *Catechism of the Catholic Church* says that homosexuals are not responsible for their condition. They do not choose this condition (n. 2358).

9

Spiritual direction and the Interindividual gay

The transition to the Interindividual stage[1]

Liebert means by the term 'Interindividual' people who are free enough to be themselves and let others be themselves fully. These are people of a high degree of social awareness. Some authors would refer to this stage of life as the 'autonomous' individual. Liebert does not use that term because in our society autonomous often refers to the kind of person who has those characteristics which are opposite to this stage. 'In our society, "autonomy" more typically connotes an enclosed, isolated, nuclear self, completely unaffected by other persons and systems.'[2] Therefore, she opts for the term 'Interindividual' as a less ambiguous expression.

I suspect that it would be rare that someone would be beginning direction who is in this transition. Usually direction will have started at an earlier stage. The director is more likely to experience a directee going through this transition during the course of working with the directee. Some of our directees never move into the Interindividual stage. Their highest level of development may have some characteristics of this transition but be lacking in others. As in the case of the transition into the Conscientious stage, this one has that liminal quality of having some of the characteristics of the previous stage and some that are more properly ascribed to the Interindividual stage.

The achievements of the Conscientious person are enhanced as the directee moves through this transition. There is even greater awareness of the self and other people. This awareness makes it possible for them to

be more tolerant of themselves and others. They are tolerant of themselves when they learn to live with their inner conflicts because they can
tolerate the existence of opposites. Toleration of paradox and contradiction during this transition will make it possible at the Interindividual
stage to enter into and negotiate the complexities of life. The director will
find that Interindividuals are very creative when it comes to the pursuit
of the spiritual life as such. That is because they can handle complexity,
paradox and the difference between their inner and outer lives. During
the transitional period there is the experience of conflict, but conflict at a
higher level. As they move through this time they will come to know and
feel the conflict between their personal freedom and their responsibilities. Conflicts which were resolved at the Conscientious level may
emerge now in a more subtle form, requiring a new resolution. The goal
of this transition is further integration. Integration now means that
process and development are not a goal, but rather a way of life. It is the
nature of transition that they be searching for the causes and reasons
for what is happening in their spiritual lives. They must possess such an
understanding of themselves in relationships and of their psychological
growth if they are to enter fully into this new level of development.

The director may have the feeling working with these directees in
such a transition that the student is passing beyond the master. And that
may be the case. I would not want to venture a guess of how many
directors are themselves in the Interindividual stage. But that does not
mean that they are becoming superfluous. It simply means that their task
will take different forms. In particular at this time their job is to help
the directee to be discriminating. Directees still need help to be able to
distinguish their outer and inner lives, the significant difference among
individuals, and how they are still dependent in certain areas of their
lives, although fully independent in others.

The transition to the Interindividual stage anticipates the stage itself
when the directee takes even more interest in the spiritual journey in
itself and not for some extraneous goal. This transition is marked by a
clearer sensitivity to social issues and a willingness to look at the issue
of intimacy in their lives honestly and without presuppositions. What
is still lacking is the full integration of any of the opposites with which
the directee has become comfortable. In the areas of freedom and
responsibility, achievement and intimacy, one more step is required.

The Interindividual stage

Many who follow the spiritual path seem to get bogged down at the Conscientious stage. While this is a high stage of development, the temptation is to remain there. Many move into this further stage because they are disillusioned with their lives, good as they are. They have a sense they are a part of something much larger than themselves. They are capable of something deeper. They want a more profound relationship with others. That is why this stage is called Interindividual. If they are at this level, they allow others to be themselves as they seek for greater mutuality with them. Because they do not approach others with their own agenda they can achieve a greater intimacy with them. Striving for the highest degree of self-appropriation possible at this level never implies a kind of isolated, self-enclosed person. If they are Inter-individual, they are interdependent with others and with all of creation, especially in the ways they can bring justice to situations which lack it.

What is so refreshing about working with Interindividual directees is their ability to tolerate ambiguity. Few things in the spiritual life can be resolved along black and white terms. The reason these people can do so much of their own direction is that they can transcend ordinary differences. Rather than getting caught in arguing about choices which seem contradictory or worrying about having to make a decision which is an either/or one, they move all consideration to a higher level. By putting individual issues in a larger context they are able to live with seeming contradiction. The kind of discernment of spirits which takes place now will be very sophisticated. Because they can contextualize personal issues in terms of the larger structures of society, sinful as many of them are, they will resolve these personal issues differently. Let us take the example of someone who has good job security, lives the life of an upper-middle-class person, and has many of the advantages of living in a developed society. He or she in their spiritual pursuit may be called to live a greater life of detachment. Some would respond by simplifying their lives by getting rid of one of their cars, not buying the latest fashion in clothes, and having no more than one TV set. In isolation this may be an admirable thing to do, but the truly Interindividual person will respond from a larger context. He/she may get rid of their summer home on the beach, but that will be irrelevant to their spiritual journey. More importantly, they will focus on how they can lobby Congress or Parliament to pass bills which are more respective of the poor. Or they may support programmes that are assisting people in developing countries to utilize their land more fully. The response to the spiritual challenge has been moved to a higher level, a more Interindividual one. Inter-individuals are world-conscious people.

This sensitivity to the larger context in no way takes away from the fact that at this level we are dealing with people who have a deep inner life. And even more heartening is the fact that they can be expressive about that inner life. They are not afraid of any of their feelings. They are comfortable with those feelings of anger and sexuality which they previously hesitated to embrace fully. The reason for this ease in accept-ing their feelings is that now their growth in the various dimensions of their lives – physical, psychological, mental, ethical, spiritual – is taking place simultaneously. At previous levels these different areas of growth tended to be more staggered.

Living at a level of higher complexity consciousness, to use the language of Teilhard de Chardin, means that Interindividuals will need to re-evaluate their earlier commitments. Not that there was anything inappropriate in those earlier commitments. They were the proper response at the time. But now the directees see themselves in a larger arena of human living. At the Conscientious stage they integrated the claiming of themselves as individuals, clearly distinguishing themselves from others. Now they want to reintegrate the others into their lives. They are seeking union, but the kind of union that Teilhard talked about when he said 'union differentiates'.

There is a generosity of spirit in Interindividuals. They know that doing the minimum required by charity or conscience is not enough. Their criteria for acting are not simply those of requirements from church, society or family, but from their own inner life. They have a broader understanding of themselves and the world around them. Since they have come to terms with themselves in a realistic way, they are able to be more compassionate and kind to themselves. Ambiguities in their inner life are accepted as part of being human. Because there is greater freedom within their inner world, elements from the un-conscious emerge more readily. As a result they may be dealing with many so-called negative feelings in direction. This may be surprising for someone who has reached such a quality of spiritual life, but those feelings which have been pushed down very deep earlier in life can-not come forth until a certain degree of freedom has been obtained by the person. Often sexual feelings will play an important role and

Interindividuals may be dealing with some aspects of their sexuality for the first time.

Reintegration is called for on all levels. The integration done at the Conscientious level is insufficient at this stage. However, we cannot presume that just because the Interindividual has a high level of spiritual development that it is without pain. Spiritual maturity brings with it its own kind of ideals and aspirations. But the spiritually mature person is also more aware of life's limitations. Some adjustment between the two must be made. If we are at this degree of maturity we need to find ways to keep our ideals alive and also engage in life fully. Dealing creatively with both sides of the tension can be disturbing.

The goal of the Interindividual is achieving harmony among groups and themselves, to transcend the differences between themselves and others. These people are the great reconcilers. They seek for reconciliation on all levels: within themselves, between their outer and inner lives, between themselves and others, between themselves and creation. Part of the reconciliation process is the matter of self-care. The kind of self-care appropriate at this stage differs from the Conscientious stage because now care for themselves is included in their caring for groups.[3] Now self-care carries with it no hint of selfishness but rather springs from the realization that it is only the healthy person who can help the other. Not only do Interindividuals know themselves in so far as they can distinguish themselves from others, but also to the degree that they can create union with others.

As we would expect, the imaging of God has a different character. Since the independent self is no longer the main concern, they may not so easily picture God as a person or along personal lines. Images of God are vague but the intimacy with God is more available. Interindividuals may be more at home with the darkness and obscurity of a John of the Cross than with the more anthropomorphic images of father, mother, saviour, creator, friend, lover. What images they do find amenable may be those of their own creation. The images will be more felt than imagined. God is like the affect or feeling we get from a poem apart from the meaning of the words or the intention of the poet. It is something they have to do on their own. Doing their own spiritual direction is part of being at this level. As these directees assume more responsibility for their spiritual lives, the director may be following more than leading.

The joy of working with Interindividuals is that these are people with a vision where the self is part of the vision. These people have great respect for others and they allow themselves to be guided by their unconscious world. Here the director will find in the directees a greater intimacy with self, others and God. These gay men and women see themselves as co-creators with God to bring about a more just world. Their inner and outer lives are in harmonious union and this is manifested in their external behaviour.

There are still areas of growth at this stage. Interindividuals will need a companion (whether spouse, friend or spiritual director) to be with them as they deal with the fact that they must live in sinful structures and institutions which are at variance with their ideals. I suspect the major challenge of this stage of adult development is what traditional Christian spirituality has called *kenosis*, self-emptying.[4] Interindividuals die to themselves when they accept the autonomy of others, when they build relationships which are truly mutual and intimate, and when they confront the sinful structures in which they find their lives entwined.[5]

Spiritual growth is still possible beyond the Interindividual stage, but these people do not need spiritual direction. Directors working with Interindividual gays need to keep the various characteristics of this stage in mind. I shall focus on three areas: the transformation of loss, the poetics of intimacy, and the public passage.

The transformation of loss

What the authors of *Coming Out Within* have to say about the transformation of loss matches very closely what is happening at the Interindividual stage.[6] There is expanded vision, greater depth of insight into other people and the ability to transcend the ordinary meaning of things in their lives. Especially appropriate for the Interindividual stage is what these authors further say:

> Paralleling this (the transformation of loss) is an increased intimacy with one's true self, with others, with the global community, and with the Spirit who weaves it all together. Up to this point in the phases of loss, the journey has been fairly solitary . . . There is a movement away from self-absorption and toward reinvolvement with the community and a deepening concern for the interconnectedness of all human beings.[7]

This wider, more comprehensive spiritual life is now possible because a great deal of integration has taken place at the Conscientious level. As a result more clarity of life-issues is now possible and there is no longer the Conformist's searching for identity nor the need to take possession of the self of the Conscientious stage. The people at the Interindividual level are now free to be open to the future. They more easily move from one symbol system to a new one. They can leave old perspectives behind. They construct new self-images as well as more images of God. They really do hand their lives over to God. 'As life images are constructed and then dismantled, the good news is that transformed loss occasions an increased willingness to surrender the ego to the Ultimate Wisdom.'[8]

These authors give several examples of gay/lesbian persons who have transformed their loss in such a way that they have a greater vision of community and of social justice, definite emphases of the Interindividual person. These are persons who have moved beyond the dependence of material possessions (the Conformist) and even of the claiming of their very personhood (the Conscientious) so that they can relish the mystical side of life. For this reason their image of God moves away from God as a person to the God beyond gender such as God-as-Energy or God-as-Wisdom.[9] Because these stories so well illustrate what I believe to be going on in the lives of Interindividual gay directees I am summarizing one of these narratives. The authors relate the following story which comes from a gay man who is at the Interindividual stage.

It is the story of Randy Blue Cloud, a native American, born a Christian, who went to a Christian boarding school in New Mexico. He was a quiet boy who was more interested in reading than in social events. He seemed different than the others. While in high school he became aware that his sexual orientation was toward other men. He had always been interested in the things of the Church and knew that he wanted to follow the calling of a holy man. After high school he went to the seminary to become a minister. Surprisingly for him, he was not happy in the seminary. The God presented to him was a strict and judgemental one which was not the image he had received at home. His teachers said that we are put on this earth to subdue it, a view that was contrary to that of his tribe. The spirituality he received emphasized the separation of the spirit and the flesh, and, of course, that homosexuals were living sinful lives and needed to be converted from that way of life.

This went against all that he sensed was true about God, nature and himself. So in order to deal with his depression he felt that he needed to follow his best instincts and he took a leave of absence from the seminary. He returned to his tribe where he reacquainted himself with their customs. He participated in their rituals such as the sweat lodge and he was open about his sexual orientation to the local medicine man. The medicine man in turn taught him about the special place gays have had in the native American tradition.[10] From him Randy learned about the sacredness of the earth and how we all are part of the Great Spirit. He was in the school of the holistic view of all creation. During his vision quest he was reminded that as a gay man he was different and this difference was a source of power.

Randy resigned from the seminary and told his former teachers that he was called to help gays and lesbians become more one with the universe. He gathered stories and put them into writing. He gave talks on college campuses on the relatedness of all things in life. He had become a holy man. Randy had to lose his first image of becoming a holy man in order to become the one he did become.[11]

This story as illustrative of the spiritual journey of the gay Inter-individual hardly needs any comment. The major themes of this stage of growth are found here in very clear ways: the movement from a received and narrow image of the spiritual to a reformulated one more in contact with nature itself, the opening up of the sources of creativity and imagination through story-telling and ritualization, the claiming of himself as gay in a larger context, the re-establishing of his cultural roots in a way in which he is both liberated and contributing to that culture, and, finally, the empowering of others to see beyond their alienation and 'disconnectedness from themselves, others and the earth to the oneness of all things'.[12] Surely, this is a gay man who has moved into the Inter-individual stage and has been transformed. As far as spiritual direction is concerned, some directors will be dealing with analogous cases and may meet such directees at different times as they go through this trans-formation. The story of Randy points out how significant counselling is at this time. What was said about his time with the tribe's medicine man and his vision quest could well be said about spiritual direction with someone moving along the path of a similar transformation. I know from experience that it is a joy to work with a modern-day gay shaman.

The poetics of intimacy[13]

I must add a few observations about the Interindividual directees and their relationships. For all, and certainly for the gay directees, personal relationships are significantly different now than they were at the

Conformist stage. Then they were viewed more superficially. They were treated in a way that Thomas Moore calls 'literalistic'. To treat someone literally means that I do not experience that person as a symbol, as a reality which has many dimensions, has many ways of being in the world. I reduce the person to a judgement that I make about him or her, and place the person in a category of people with little regard for individual differences. At the Interindividual level directees have acquired what Moore calls the 'poetics of intimacy'. What this means in brief is that now the gay person can meet others as they are, treating them in all their diversity and 'reading' them in a multidimensional way. Moore says:

> We might first recognize that a person is a text of sorts, as are his or her stories, theories, ideas, memories, wishes intentions – anything that a person expresses. Like any rich text, a person has many, many layers of meaning, most of them unknown even to himself.[14]

In other words, in the area of intimacy the Interindividual person is a *hermeneut*, someone who knows how to interpret the experiential life of another. That is, now gay persons meet others in relationships as they would meet a work of art. They do not try to understand the other person, whether lover, friend or acquaintance, through analysis or their own expectations of what a relationship should provide for them. Rather the intimate one is a voice to which they listen and try to understand. Just as we do not understand a literary work through a scientific kind of knowing but rather 'through an historical encounter which calls forth personal experience of being here in the world',[15] so gay people listen to the words of those who love them, 'I love you', as a poetic expression. 'I love you' is not equated with 'I want to have sex with you' or 'I want you to fulfil my needs' or 'I want you to take care of me' or 'I want you to fill up my emptiness'. Moore points out that such expressions as 'I love you' are 'open to reflection, discussion, change and emphasis. The poetics of a relationship are an aspect of its mystery; we never know fully the whys and wherefores of our thoughts and emotions.'[16] Gay Interindividual men and women meet the person who loves them as an embodiment of this mystery, someone with whom they can symbolically interact, never exhausting what is available for them.

In the language of contemporary hermeneutics we are not talking about a loving encounter as we would meet a text (the text being the person who loves us). That would simply be two people meeting only in terms of what they find attractive in each other. That is to be literalistic, according to Moore. Nor do we encounter each other in terms of the world behind the text, that is, the background, the parents, the cultural upbringing of the one who loves us. We may fall in love with someone's background or culture, but that is not to love the person as such. Rather, we encounter the world in front of the text, that is, the new reality which is being created in this very encounter. Gay persons and those who love them are both being changed in the encounters they have. Such poetic openness will allow gay directees to relate to the person who is there for them as the paintings are there waiting to be seen or the music is there waiting to be performed, played and heard. Moore puts it this way:

> By letting our imaginations be saturated with imagery that is moving, thought-provoking, instructive, and wise, we bring to our close relationships a mind and heart open to variety in human expression, individuality, eccentricity, pathos, joy, and the whole round of emotions.[17]

This is at the opposite end of cruising, going to gay bars for a pick-up, having sex before we even think about beginning a relationship.[18] The director might find such activity at the Conformist level, although usually those things indicate an even lesser stage of development. But at the Interindividual level gays connect deeply with men and women meeting them at their own depth, where their experience of God meets theirs. The beloved, and in this case the person who loves the gay directee, is like an icon. We, the viewers, do not look at the icon, the icon looks at us and it is as if the essence of God is shining through the icon from behind, and passing through it this spiritual reality comes into our own hearts. As a director my advice to a gay directee, at all three stages of development, who is looking for a relationship is simple: *Look where you are not looking*. Usually, the best love for us, like the icon, is looking at us, but we cannot see it because we are too preoccupied looking for what we think we want. We need to stop and let ourselves be seen. If the director will ask the directees about the people who love them rather than the people they love or would like to love, the two will find a great deal of material for further reflection. This is especially true at the Interindividual stage. Perhaps, only at this level of development can gay men and women commit themselves to someone so they may love that person, rather than demanding the presence of love before they make their commitment.[19]

The public passage[20]

Just as I have linked the interior passage to the Conformist stage and the passage into intimacy to the Conscientious stage, so I see this third passage as the task of many who are at the Interindividual stage. This public passage is coming out as gay and as Christian in their work and the community at large. The Whiteheads say that this passage is not for everyone. I would agree and say that to be at the Interindividual level does not mean that one will come out in a fully public way. On the other hand, it is Interindividual gays who will best negotiate such a public passage.[21] If gay men or women decide to come out fully, at this level they are not doing it to be exhibitionists. Most probably they see it connected with their concern for justice issues, as their way to bring greater humanization to our society, as their contribution to the recreation of our world. Also, if they want to be role models for other gay men and women, they will need to become more public about their sexual orientation.

I believe that the Whiteheads correctly identify what is the best of all motivations for coming out, namely, to be generative. It is the gays' way of parenting. Generativity is one of the characteristics of the Interindividual stage. Often people will move into this stage fully at about the time in their lives when they are ready to be role models and to leave something for the next generation. What we so lack at this time is a good model of homosexual Christian maturing. We need the modelling of a gay Christian male and female to present to our world that it is possible to be not only gay and Christian but also to be gay, Christian and spiritually mature.[22]

One of the areas where therapy and spiritual direction may differ is that in the latter situation as the directees grow spiritually, they are expected to be more community-orientated, more focused on issues that move beyond their personal world. They must have a mission. Their lives should have a prophetic quality about them. Perhaps, this public passage is a way for them to find this mission. This will not be possible if they remain in the closet. 'A certain public exposure and light is required for this virtue of generativity to have its effect.'[23] Perhaps, the greatest and final challenge of any who follow the spiritual path, Christian or not, is that moment when they must decide between the good and the greater good, between what is needed and the greater need. I suspect most directors working with Interindividual directees will experience that moment in many of their directees' lives. Finally, we can only say that it is a grace given to some. To move into the interior life to discover who I am and what are my qualities, to become a friend to myself so I can love myself, is not optional. It is implied in the evangelical call to love God and our neighbour as we love ourselves. Nor is the passage to intimacy an option. Intimacy with others follows upon self-intimacy. We do not become close to ourselves without also becoming close to others. One automatically follows upon the other, else we make a mockery of the meaning of self-intimacy, turning it into a kind of selfishness. But this third passage requires an invitation. Both director and directee can only wait to see if such an invitation will be proffered. I include one more example from *Coming Out Within* which for me highlights this movement into the public arena as a way of being generative and parenting the next generation. This is a story about surrendering oneself to God.[24]

Grant was a body-builder *par excellence*. He spent a great part of his life exercising and sculpting his physique into the beautiful ideal he had of what the male body could be. It would not be too much to say that he worshipped this ideal body and it was his cult. He idolized his own body. But he could not figure out why he could not get a lover. There were plenty of people who wanted a one-night stand with that body beautiful, but no more. One of those times Grant became a victim of violence with the result that he was crippled for life. He would never walk again despite his best efforts. He went into a deep depression. No more perfect body for him, so what was left in life? He became very vulnerable and frightened and broke down in the hospital. The Jewish rabbi talked with him and told Grant his own tale of wanting perfection but not achieving it and how this had transformed his life.

Grant left the hospital a very different man. He set up a small appliance repair store in his garage but, more importantly,

> He learned to see beyond the body and derived strength from the disabled children he helped coach for the Special Olympics. By squarely facing his own fear of physical imperfection, he was able to transcend his disability and to accept whatever God had in store for him.[25]

And what God had in store for Grant was passing on his life to those disabled children and enriching their lives by mentoring them.

Grant's story reminds me of the number of gays with whom I have worked who have (or have had) this great longing for the perfect body and who never quite achieved it. There are a number of variations on this theme. Some gays are in fact quite handsome people but do not recognize it themselves either out of fear or poor self-acceptance. Others who might belong to what we call 'the beautiful people' are quite manipulative about their physical endowments although they have little consciousness of their being so. Some have a sense of the sacramentality of their bodies whether they have the desired body form or not. In my experience these are few. The first step in integrating this longing in the directees' spiritual lives is to help them appreciate the human body in terms of the beauty of human form and not just as an object of erotic interest. There is no better symbol of human sensibility than the human body itself. For an Interindividual person the physically attractive and the sacramental are rarely separate. And, more importantly, the physically unattractive person is also a sacrament for them.

The second step is to assist gay directees to accept their call to being generative for others and that generativity has nothing to do with physical beauty. The slim waist will bring love to no one. If we take care of ourselves physically, it should be for health, not romance. To be the one for another who is a guide through difficult moments in life, an inspiration when there is discouragement, and the trusted friend when everyone else fails is to achieve an intimacy with another person not given by physical intimacy alone. In fact, admiration of pure physical beauty can be alienating because the interaction is not fully human. How many times have we met someone to whom we were instantly physically attracted and found upon meeting them that they were boring, biased, superficial and lacking in character. True mentors bring their confidants to a level of personal intimacy and appreciation of their beauty, both inner and outer, in a way that people with whom they might be physically intimate cannot. Such mentoring, appreciation of authentic beauty, and finding beauty in love rather than love in the beautiful are all signs of moving into the Interindividual stage.

All passages involve some rite of passage. In the passage to the interior life the rite is purely personal. In the passage into intimacy the rite is semi-public, that is, it is public on a limited basis. But for this third passage, the rite must be more fully public. Grant made this rite of passage when he found the meaning of his life in the disabled children he coached. At the present time such rites of passage for Interindividual gays and lesbians, while more public in character, will not be fully public. Most churches at the present time do not allow the celebration of what might be called a homosexual union. This is not a realistic rite of passage because to be so demands more public acknowledgement. But there are other forms of a more public rite of passage such as being members of committees for gay/lesbian rights, participating in the Campaign for Human Development, or something like going to and acting in gay and lesbian movies and plays.[26] There is the simple fact of the presence of gays in the arts and all other professions.[27] There are gay members of Congress and state legislatures. Many Interindividual gays will be prepared to participate in one or other of these rites of passage and the director will need to work with them both in terms of supporting them as well as challenging them as regards their true intentions. Although it may not seem this way to many gays, the churches are in the process of facilitating some of these rites of public passage. The Whiteheads remark:

> In acknowledging the existence of and then creating public space for homosexual Catholics to stand in the community, the Church facilitates this third, public passage. In doing this the Church senses, though not without some anxiety and self-doubt, that it is these maturing gay and lesbian Christians who will witness to believers the shape of homosexual holiness.[28]

John McNeill gives several examples of how homosexuals make contributions to the human community by their service. He points out that not only have gays and lesbians contributed in the area of the arts but also to positions such as teachers, social workers, hospital orderlies and nurses, student counsellors, psychologists, clergy persons and many other occupations.[29] He says:

> It is my belief that the presence of the lesbian and gay community within the human community is essential to its human development. Gays are the oil that keeps the whole machine running smoothly. This is so true that if, somehow, suddenly there were no gay people, the human community would be in serious jeopardy.[30]

I am in complete agreement with that statement and so I end where I began, that homosexuality is one of God's most significant gifts to humanity.

Notes

1 As with the previous two stages I begin with a summary of the work of Elizabeth Liebert in her formulation of this stage. I believe my summary is faithful to her thought, although I often rearticulate it. For a fuller treatment of this level of adult development, see Chapter VII of her book, *Changing Life Patterns: Adult Development in Spiritual Direction* (New York: Paulist Press, 1992).

2 *Ibid.*, p. 121.

3 For a discussion of the dimensions of comprehensive communal care for gays and lesbians see Chapter 6, 'Affirmation, advocacy, and opposition', Larry Kent Graham, *Discovering Images of God* (Louisville, KY: Westminster/John Knox Press, 1997).

4 For a further explanation of this term see 'Kenosis' in Michael Downey (ed.), *The New Dictionary of Catholic Spirituality*, (Collegeville, MN: The Liturgical Press, 1993), p. 584. There it states: 'For some modern spiritual writers, *kenosis* has been used as a term to refer to the process of self-transcendence called for in authentic conversion of heart.'

5 In a personal note to me Xavier Seubert kindly wrote: 'With the concept of "Interindividual" you create a sacramental space. By that I mean that all the energies, which normally get diverted into cults of narcissism, bar cruising, adulation of the body beautiful and muscle queens, are given the space and, hence, the opportunity to become transformed into a life-giving and generative power. What is so helpful is that you provide names and images for what is ordinarily only implicitly intuited. That further means that these powers can be related to and dialogued with.' For a discussion about homosexuality and human liberation see Mario Mieli, *Homosexuality and Liberation: Elements of a Gay Critique*, trans. David Fernbach (London: Gay Men's Press, 1980).

6 Craig O'Neill and Katherine Ritter, *Coming Out Within* (HarperSanFrancisco, 1992), see Chapter 10.

7 *Ibid.*, p. 179.

8 *Ibid.*, p. 180.

9 A great deal of feminist theology has moved in this direction. Scholarship has advanced so far in this area that I can no more than suggest two outstanding books in this area, Elizabeth A. Johnson, *She Who Is: The Mystery of God in Feminist Theological Discourse* (New York: Crossroad, 1992) and Elisabeth Schüssler Fiorenza, *In Memory of Her: A Feminist Theological Reconstruction of Christian Origins* (New York: Crossroad, 1983). For a specific application of this thought to Christ, I suggest an accessible book, Jann Aldredge-Clanton, *In Search of the Christ-Sophia: An Inclusive Christology for Liberating Christians* (Mystic, CT: Twenty-third Publications, 1995).

10 For an excellent study of the berdache tradition in Native American culture see Walter L. Williams, *The Spirit and the Flesh* (Boston; Beacon Press, 1992). Some Native American cultures venerated the berdache, androgynous people who were classified as neither men nor women.

11 O'Neill and Ritter, *Coming Out Within*, pp. 181ff.

12 *Ibid.*, p. 184.

13   This title and the following material is indebted to Thomas Moore, *Soul Mates* (New York: HarperCollins, 1994).

14   *Ibid.*, p. 245.

15   Richard E. Palmer, *Hermeneutics* (Evanston: Northwestern University Press, 1969), p. 10. For someone who would like to be introduced to the field of hermeneutics I recommend this book. It is remarkable in its clarity.

16   Moore, *Soul Mates*, p. 245.

17   *Ibid.*, p. 246.

18   I am writing this section on 5 May. As is my wont I was reading the assigned selection in Amy E. Dean, *Proud To Be: Daily Meditations for Lesbians and Gay Men* (New York: Bantam Books, 1994). I quote from the selection for 5 May:

> There's a joke in the gay and lesbian community about how to date: on the first date, you sleep with someone; on the second date, you put your possessions in a U-Haul and drive to that person's house; and on the third date, you exchange commitment vows . . .

The reflection continues urging gays and lesbians to take time with their relationships and to connect with several people so that they may learn what they want in a committed relationship. It continues:

> What the time and patience required in the process of 'seeing what's out there' can teach you is that **love is generally slow to develop. However, love *will* result when you're able to make a conscious, considerate, and mutual decision to commit to someone else.** (I use bold text for emphasis)

19   Perhaps this is not the most theologically accurate way to put the matter. Can love and commitment be separated in experience? It does make the point, however, that I do not have to feel romantic love before I can consider commitment. Many would disagree with me on this point. I am not suggesting that true committed love is not found at the Conscientious stage, but I think the quality of the commitment at the Interindividual level is more comprehensive, more springing from the unconscious resources of the person, and less focused on the other to the exclusion of others.

20   This is the third passage described by the Whiteheads in their article 'Three passages to maturity', in Robert Nugent (ed.), *A Challenge to Love* (New York: Crossroad, 1986), pp. 183ff. John O'Neill in Chapter 8 of *Freedom, Glorious Freedom* adds some of his own observations to the meaning of this third passage.

21   I fully concur with the Whiteheads when they say: 'The special challenge of this third passage argues that we enter it only when strengthened by the awareness and support gained over the years that are usually involved in making the earlier passages' ('Three passages to maturity', p.185).

22   *Ibid.*, p. 184.

23   *Ibid.*, p. 184. As a friend, Peter Gray, puts it: 'People do not light a fire and put it under a bushel basket (or in the closet).'

24   Craig O'Neill and Katherine Ritter, *Coming Out Within*, pp. 194ff. Again, I summarize the story in my own words.

25   *Ibid.*, p. 197. Some of the other examples the authors give are like topic sentences in a description of the lives of Interindividual gay and lesbian persons: moving from

meaningless to mentoring, connecting life with death, being reborn to empathy, healing into wholeness.

26   Those gays who wish to get involved in community-building issues might contact *Communications* (P.O. Box 10658, Chicago, IL. 60610–0658). This is a newsletter whose purpose is 'dialogue on the relationship between personal sexuality, spirituality and ministry for the purpose of building community among lesbians, gays and bi-sexual clergy and religious and friends'.

27   Recently, the presence of lesbians in TV programmes has become more acceptable. Gay men on TV at the present time cannot come out as easily. Apparently, while some straight men might be intrigued by lesbians, they are still very threatened by the presence of gay men.

28   *Ibid.*, p. 186. Statements such as the one by the Roman Catholic bishops of the United States about parents accepting, loving and assisting their gay and lesbian children contribute to making this public space for homosexuals.

29   McNeill, *Freedom, Glorious Freedom*, Chapter 9, gives an example of coming out by means of a covenant union (a phrase he prefers to gay marriage). For a challenging presentation of the contribution of the gay experience to theology and spirituality, especially in terms of friendship, see *Just Good Friends: Towards a Lesbian and Gay Theology of Relationships* by Elizabeth Stuart (London: Mowbray, 1995).

30   *Ibid.*, p. 81.

Epilogue

Rarely does one book cover adequately the topic to which it is devoted. Although I have tried to focus on what I consider the main issues that arise in the situation of spiritual direction with gay people who are serious about the spiritual pursuit, there are areas left untouched. I make reference to but one of these areas, that of the cultural similarities and differences among gays and lesbians. As is obvious, good directors treat each person as a valued individual precisely as individual. But the cultural nuances may escape them unless they themselves have been sensitized to the ethnicity of the directee if it is different from their own. Our shared common humanity does not erase these cultural differences. For instance, those from an ethnic group which tends to deny the presence of homosexuality in their group and/or which places primary importance on heterosexual marriage and having children may find it more difficult to come to terms with their homosexuality and/or coming out to family members. At this point I can do no more than give spiritual directors some references where they may find additional resources for their own education in this matter. Not all these references are to fully developed studies of the cultural variety of gays. We must await further research in this area.

In *One More River to Cross: Black and Gay in America*[1] Keith Boykin addresses what it means to be black and gay in the United States with its history of racism. Homosexuality is not just a white thing and blacks are not more homophobic than whites. He makes the point that 'By critically examining racism and distinguishing it from homophobia, they (African Americans) conclude that the latter is a river that need not be crossed.'[2] Boykin does not agree. Another book peculiar to the US is *Living the*

Spirit: A Gay American Indian Anthology[3] compiled by gay American Indians with Will Roscoe as the co-ordinating editor. This collection of stories, essays and poems provides an understanding of what it means to be gay and Native American.

More has been written on the Latino and/or Spanish-speaking gay person. *Latin American Male Homosexualities,*[4] edited by Stephen O. Murray, is a serious anthology of anthropological studies which indicates the complexities and riches of Latin American gay men. Of special interest may be the essays dealing with homosexual categorization, *machismo* and homosexuality, the *activo-pasivo* cultural dichotomy, and the gay movement and human rights. *Muy Macho: Latino Men Confront Their Manhood*[5] is another anthology edited by Ray Gonzalez. This time the essays are by well-known Hispanic authors. It is a study of *machismo* by men talking about themselves in terms of the perception of Latino men as 'virile and brash, full of passion and testosterone'. The writers address the question of whether Latino men can 'redefine the macho myth without abandoning the positive role models they have. In other words, can Latin men do away with the myth of aggressive yet emotionally private males and still prosper?'[6] Emile L. Bergmann and Paul Julian Smith have edited a large volume of essays called *¿Entiendes? Queer Readings, Hispanic Writings.*[7] This is a scholarly exploration of gay and lesbian identity in Spanish-speaking cultures against the background of contemporary queer theory. It is a major contribution. *De Los Otros: Intimacy and Homosexuality Among Mexican Men*[8] by Joseph Carrier is a specialized study limiting itself to one group of Hispanics.

> A major premise of mine has been that most Mexican men who have other men as primary or secondary sexual partners are able over time to come to terms with homosexual behaviors which, although legal in Mexico, are still considered reprehensible and deviant in their society. My study has therefore focused on learning about the coping strategies, lifestyles, and sexual behaviors of ordinary men (that is, men not in psychotherapy or institutionalized settings) who are actively involved in homosexual encounters.[9]

Two books have appeared that are helpful for introducing one to the Asian gay and lesbian experience. *A Lotus of Another Color: An Unfolding of the South Asian Gay and Lesbian Experience*, edited by Rakesh Ratti.[10] This collection of stories and poems speaks of the pain of the coming-out process in South Asian countries. *Asian American Sexualities: Dimensions of the Gay and Lesbian Experience*[11] edited by Russell Leong addresses a variety of issues by a large number of authors. All deal with the various nuances in the way that race and sexuality intersect with each other in the lives of gays, lesbians and bisexual Asian Americans.

Other specific topics for which some writing and research is available include the very well researched *Gay and Gray: The Older Homosexual Man* by Raymond M. Berger;[12] *Camping by a Billabong*, a collection of gay and lesbian stories from Australian history by Robert French;[13] and 'Gayness and God' by Rabbi Yaakov Levado, an Orthodox gay rabbi, which studies the struggle between personal identity and the Hebrew scriptures.[14] *Men of Color: A Context for Service to Homosexually Active Men*,[15] edited by John F. Longres, contains essays that deal not only with the already mentioned African/American, Latino and Native American gays but additional ones dealing with Filipino and Korean gay men. Finally, *Same Sex, Different Cultures* by Gilbert Herdt[16] is a study of patterns of same-gender relations both in ancient and in contemporary cultures. This wide-ranging book shows that homosexuality has been an integral part of many of this world's cultures and that homosexuality is not always to be seen as something idiosyncratic to a society.[17]

Of all the things written here, the one that is most worthy to serve as the concluding note is the giftedness of being gay or lesbian. This difference in how one is drawn to others, this other way of loving, this distinct form of religious sensibility will continue to be what it always has been: filling up with a greater wholeness the beauty of humanity. Gay/lesbian presence in the churches will be the catalyst for some of the more imaginative theological reflection and expression in the future. Spiritual direction with the gay person is ultimately about this giftedness. It may be that more time in the sessions is spent on issues of hurt, pain, suffering, integrating one's sexuality with one's bodiliness, or dealing with one's inner call to love and what religious denominations ask of their gay and lesbian members. But the giftedness of being a homosexual must be ever present like background music. However, if my experience can be accepted as a proper source of information here, then more time in spiritual direction with gays and lesbians will devoted to their issues as human beings rather than as gays and lesbians specifically. What distinguishes men from women, one race from another, and gays/lesbians from straights is not the most significant part of us. What we hold in common is. Still, for gays and lesbians to grasp fully the humanity they share with heterosexuals, it will necessary for them to dwell in all the possibilities of their giftedness.

Bill Huebsch in his poetic/prose reflection entitled, 'What does it mean for lesbian or gay people to know Jesus?' sees the process by which gays journey to greater union with God as similar to Jesus' raising Lazarus from the dead.

> Gay men and lesbians will tell you plainly
> > that their way of loving
> > comes as 'naturally' to them
> > as straight men and women
> > > understand their attractions.
>
> Lesbians and gay men will tell you
> > that the truth is this:
> > sexuality is a gift from God
> > and homosexuality is one expression
> > > of that gift.
>
> That's the truth
> > that has set so many
> > lesbians and gay men free at last.
>
> That's the truth that has brought them
> > out of the closet of hiding,
> > > out of the tombs.
>
> And in this coming out,
> > gay men and lesbians often say that,
> > for the first time,
> > > it is now clear
> > > how God touches us with eternal truth.[18]

Spiritual directors, by recognizing and calling forth the homosexual giftedness of their directees, call them out of their tombs. Hopefully, the journey that the director and directee make together will make it possible for the gay person to move out of hiding into the light and to move from unfreedom to freedom. The whole work of spiritual direction with gays and lesbians is encapsulated in the cry of Jesus as the still bound Lazarus emerges from the darkness: *'Unbind him and let him go!'*[19]

Notes

1 Keith Boykin, *One More River to Cross: Black and Gay in America* (New York: Doubleday: Anchor Books, 1996). The author seems unfamiliar with the Roman Catholic tradition. He calls religious orders 'religious sects' and he misunderstands the purpose of marriage as presently articulated by the Roman Catholic Church (p. 138).

2 *Ibid.*, p. 262. See also Catherine E. McKinley and L. Joyce DeLaney, *Afrekete: An Anthology of Black Lesbian Writing* (New York: Anchor Books, 1995).

3 Will Roscoe (ed.), *Living the Spirit: A Gay American Indian Anthology* (New York: St. Martin's Press, 1988).

4 Stephen O. Murray (ed.), *Latin American Male Homosexualities* (Albuquerque: University of New Mexico Press, 1995).

5 Ray Gonzalez, *Muy Macho: Latino Men Confront Their Manhood* (New York: Doubleday: Anchor Books, 1996).

6 *Ibid.*, p. xv.

7 Emile L. Bergman and Paul Julian Smith, *¿Entiendes? Queer Readings, Hispanic Writings* (Durham, NC: Duke University Press, 1995). The Spanish word, ¿Entiendes? literally means 'Do you understand?', figuratively means 'Are you queer?'

8 Joseph Carrier, *De Los Otros: Intimacy and Homosexuality Among Mexican Men* (New York: Columbian University Press, 1995).

9 *Ibid.*, p. xvii.

10 Rakesh Ratti (ed.), *A Lotus of Another Color: An Unfolding of the South Asian Gay and Lesbian Experience*, (Boston: Alyson Publications, Inc., 1993).

11 Russell Leong, *Asian American Sexualities: Dimensions of the Gay and Lesbian Experience* (New York and London: Routledge, 1996).

12 Raymond M. Berger, *Gay and Gray: The Older Homosexual Man* (New York and London: Harrington Park Press, 1996).

13 Robert French, *Camping by a Billabong* (Sydney: BlackWattle Press, 1993).

14 This essay is found in *Beyond Queer: Challenging Gay Left Orthodoxy*, a reader edited by Bruce Bawer (New York: The Free Press, 1996), pp. 194ff. Although one cannot make universal statements about gay and lesbian Jews based on this article alone, I would imagine that it could be very helpful for an individual Jew who is homosexual.

15 John F. Longres, *Men of Color: A Context for Service to Homosexually Active Men* (New York: Harrington Park Press, 1996). See also Hilda Hidalgo, *Lesbians of Color: Social and Human Services* (Binghamton, NY: The Haworth Press, 1995).

16 Gilbert Herdt, *Same Sex, Different Cultures* (Boulder, CO, and Oxford: Westview Press, 1997). For a discussion of the terms, gay and queer, and their differences see page 8 and following. See also the section called 'The cultural history of homosexuality' (p. 38 and following).

17 The wide-ranging series of essays in Michael Lowenthal (ed.), *Sex, Spirit, Community: Gay Men at the Millennium* (New York: Jeremy P. Tarcher, 1997), include several from a specifically cultural point of view.

18 Bill Huebsch, *A Radical Guide for Catholics: Rooted in the Essentials of Our Faith* (Mystic, CT: Twenty-third Publications, 1992), p. 134.
19 *Ibid.*, p. 135.

Index